U.S. POLICY AFTER RUSSIA'S ESCALATION IN SYRIA

HEARING

BEFORE THE

COMMITTEE ON FOREIGN AFFAIRS
HOUSE OF REPRESENTATIVES

ONE HUNDRED FOURTEENTH CONGRESS

FIRST SESSION

NOVEMBER 4, 2015

Serial No. 114–116

Printed for the use of the Committee on Foreign Affairs

Available via the World Wide Web: http://www.foreignaffairs.house.gov/ or
http://www.gpo.gov/fdsys/

U.S. GOVERNMENT PUBLISHING OFFICE

97–460PDF   WASHINGTON : 2015

CONTENTS

U.S. POLICY AFTER RUSSIA'S ESCALATION IN SYRIA

WEDNESDAY, NOVEMBER 4, 2015

House of Representatives,
Committee on Foreign Affairs,
Washington, DC.

The committee met, pursuant to notice, at 10:08 a.m., in room 2172 Rayburn House Office Building, Hon. Edward Royce (chairman of the committee) presiding.

Chairman ROYCE [presiding]. This hearing will come to order.

So, this hearing is on U.S. policy after Russia's escalation in Syria. It is now nearly 5 years into the Syrian conflict. That conflict has claimed more than ¼ million lives. There are 4 million people right now that have been driven from their homes in Syria. Now, through it all, the administration's response has been tepid. It has been a series of steps that were micromanaged by the White House that were very ineffectual. When I say "ineffectual," we had a situation here where we had hearings during the time, a 1-year period in which as ISIS began to move out of Raqqah, Syria and take major cities, during that period of time, as we were calling for airstrikes, as our Ambassador in Baghdad was calling for airstrikes, there were 14 major cities that fell to ISIS, fell at a time when in pickup trucks on an open desert road these were clear targets that could have been taken out.

But a choice was made. Sometimes indecision, the decision not to make a decision, is itself a choice. The choice was made in the United States not to stop ISIS then, when it could have been stopped. And the choice was also made not to arm the Kurds. Three trips out here by the Foreign Minister of Kurdistan asking for the anti-tank weapons, the artillery, the long-range mortars that they needed. Thirty percent of their troops, 30 percent of their brigades are women, females, fighting on the frontlines against ISIS on a 600-mile front. And the decision was made not to arm them.

So, ISIS now stands where it stands gaining ground as a result of our failure to act. Today the President still hasn't put forward the broad, overarching strategy needed to defeat this brutal movement, this movement of terrorists and, frankly, to secure vital U.S. national security interests here. But, instead, it is now Russia that is taking the decisive role in shaping Syria's future and not in a helpful way. Putin saw Assad losing ground. So, Russian jets have teamed up with the Iranian ground forces to solidify the Syrian dictator, and the focus of the Russian and Iranians' joint offensive is not ISIS. It is not their strongholds, but it is the opposition forces backed by the United States and Saudi Arabia.

Russian bombs, according to the NGO groups that report on this, they say over half of the Russian attacks have now been on civilian targets. Russian bombs have flattened markets, schools, villages. And the Russians at one point were bombing more targets, more targets, in one solitary day than we hit in a month and our air campaign there is even more anemic, for those of you that have followed what has happened as a consequence of Russia moving into these operations. The administration claims that it lacks targets. Yet, the special forces it is sending to Syria won't even be spotting targets. Russian attacks on the opposition and the slowdown in coalition airstrikes has actually allowed ISIS now to gain territory. ISIS is expanding. Let no one be under the delusion that Russia is focused on ISIS.

While the President characterizes Russia's moves as a sign of weakness, it is Assad who is growing stronger. Moscow's efforts show no sign of slowing. Russian cargo aircraft have been seen running Iranian weapons into Syria, a violation of the U.N. arms embargo, a violation that I assume is not going to be called to attention or challenged. But it is a clear violation of that agreement at the United Nations.

This is especially troubling as we begin another attempt to restart talks between the regime and the opposition on a new constitution and elections, and here is why: Russia claims its goal is a united secular and democratic Syria, but its efforts to prop up the Assad regime prove otherwise. How do we expect the opposition to sign onto any sort of ceasefire as long as Russia and Iran are demanding that Assad, who has murdered over 200,000 civilians? For those of us in this hearing room, we have heard in the past Caesar come forward with his photographs that he took, 50,000 photographs, of people tortured by the regime. That kind of conduct by this regime means it has lost all legitimacy with the Syrian people. So, the Russian plan is to have him stay in power and to ask at the outset that he stays in power. The statement from Vienna didn't even demand that that Assad regime stop using crude barrel bombs, some filled with chlorine gas, against civilians. That would have been a minimum step that the Russians could have supported. But their planes, they provided the air force originally to Assad.

So, a diplomatic solution is only possible with a strong, coherent, moderate opposition that can serve as a bridge from Assad to a new post-conflict government. Yet, the administration has done little to help the opposition. Its feeble train and equip program is now defunct. Washington bureaucracy and over-deference to the Shia-led Iraqi Government has held up desperately-needed weapons shipments to the Kurds, and no one believes Friday's announcement of 50 special forces will be decisive.

Ultimately, it is President Obama's responsibility tp step up and outline a plan to engage our partners and allies and bring stability to the Middle East. He is the Commander-in-Chief, but here is where I would start. As I have already said, we have urged for the longest time: Decisive airstrikes against ISIS. We have urged for the longest time: The arming of the Kurdish and Yazidi men and women out there on the frontlines with the weapons they need to turn back ISIS.

If we want an opposition to negotiate from a position of strength, why not help create sanctuary areas in Syria? This would help the Syrian people escape both the Assad regime and the Islamic State. This would also allow for more effective humanitarian relief and even slow the exodus of refugees.

We must also push back on Russia and Iran's destabilizing intervention in this conflict, and that means passing tough new sanctions on Iran's terrorist proxy, Hezbollah, because it is Hezbollah that is taking over homes in this region that used to be inhabited by Sunnis, as the ethic cleansing continues. So, we need to pass that legislation, as the House has done, and take action to uphold the U.N. arms embargo on Iran in the face of Russian violations.

Everyone but the White House seems to know the status quo cannot stand. General David Petraeus recently testified to Congress that ''Syria is a geopolitical Chernobyl and, like a nuclear disaster, the fallout from the meltdown of Syria threatens to be with us for decades,'' he said, ''and the longer it is permitted to continue, the more severe the damage will be.'' Those were his words.

I will now turn to the Democratic side for any opening statement. Yes, Lois.

Ms. FRANKEL. Thank you very much. Thank you, Mr. Royce.

And I thank the witnesses for being here today. I know you're going to be able to well handle the questions that are going to be asked you.

Mr. Chair, I wanted to just express a little different point of view. First of all, I want to say this, Mr. Chair: Thank you for this hearing. I think you have raised some very good questions and you have expressed the great frustration that a lot of us feel about Syria. I mean, it is horrific what is going on.

But, I mean, some people would say that ISIS or Daesh, whatever we call them today, came about not because of something President Obama did, but, I mean, there are some who would argue that it was the previous administration's decision to go into Iraq erroneously that started this mess that we see there today with a failed occupation of Iraq, a new government that was not inclusive. You have a void, and then, you see ISIS come from that void.

But I do want to say this: I don't want to play the blame game. That is what some people say. But I think what is important now is just to focus on the here and now and what we need to do.

This mess in Syria and the Middle East is not the fault of our President. There is a lot of blame to go around, but I am going to put it on terrorists more than the President of the United States.

I will be very interested in hearing what our two witnesses have to say.

Thank you, Mr. Chair.

Mr. KEATING. Will the gentlelady yield?

Ms. FRANKEL. Yes.

Mr. KEATING. Thank you.

We have time left, the opening statement time, and I just want to set a framework here as we have this discussion.

I will say this with the administration and, frankly, with the critics of the administration: I, for one, did not see the value of pursuing with a vetting of the Syrian rebel army. I can say that myself, looking at what happened.

But the one thing I want to have emphasized in this hearing is that you can't things both ways. You can't say we should be putting in U.S. troops on the ground there, and you can't do that and do even a modicum of security for those troops unless you are willing to hold that troop and have a huge investment of our troops.

So, the people that say the President didn't come in and he should have come in with troops, you just can't come in, drop them in, pull them out. We didn't have intelligence on the ground in Syria to make that safe for those troops that the time.

No. 2, we have to be prepared for those people that say that, that those troops have to have the support of tens of thousands of other troops. So, let's not have it in this hearing both ways. If you are going to take that tack with the President, you have to be able to say, ''Well, I support ground troops for the long term,'' tens of thousands on the ground, because you can't put them in there without supporting them safety.

So, I hope when we have this discussion today, we bear that in mind. If people have that opinion, then I respect their opinion, but I don't think that that is the best thing for our country at this time.

And I yield back.

Chairman ROYCE. Thank you, Mr. Keating.

I would like to make it clear that that is not the opinion of the members of this committee. What the members of this committee called for, for a full year of indecisive action, was the use of our air power; was a memory that we had had 116,000 airstrikes during the first Gulf War against 42 divisions of Saddam Hussein. These were armored divisions, many of them, and that it was very successful during the invasion of Kuwait.

What we called for here was not the introduction of U.S. brigades. What we called here was for the President of the United States to use the authority he had in order to take out the beginning of insurrection that started in pickup trucks. And if you can take out armored divisions, you could certainly from the air take out pickup trucks from the open desert.

And the frustration that I am expressing is over the fact that for 1 year nothing was done, as city after city fell to this marauding terrorist organization.

But I should transition to the witnesses today.

But it is partly that frustration and it is partly with meeting time after time on a bipartisan basis with the Kurdish and the Yazidi opposition asking for arms and being denied the arms to defend themselves. Those are the issues I am speaking to.

But, at this time, I would like to go to Ambassador Anne Patterson, Assistant Secretary of State of Near Eastern Affairs. She is a career member of the Senior Foreign Service and previously Ambassador Patterson served in multiple posts, including Egypt and Pakistan, and as Assistant Secretary of State for International Narcotics and Law Enforcement Affairs.

And then, to Ambassador Victoria Nuland, before assuming her position as Assistant Secretary for the Bureau of European and Eurasian Affairs at the Department of State, Ambassador Nuland served as the Department of State's spokesperson. She also served as the United States permanent representative to the North Atlantic Treaty Organization from 2005 to 2008, focusing heavily on NATO Russia issues.

Without objection, the witnesses' full prepared statements will be made part of the record, and the members here will have 5 calendar days to submit any statements or questions or extraneous material for the record.

Ambassador Patterson, if you could begin?

STATEMENT OF THE HONORABLE ANNE W. PATTERSON, ASSISTANT SECRETARY, BUREAU OF NEAR EASTERN AFFAIRS, U.S. DEPARTMENT OF STATE

Ambassador PATTERSON. Thank you, Mr. Chairman, members of the committee. Thank you for the opportunity to appear before you today to explain our strategy for resolving the devastating conflict in Syria and defeating ISIL there.

Coming after the President's decision to intensify the campaign against ISIL and Secretary Kerry's meetings in Vienna, the design of a path forward for a political transition, this hearing is particularly well-timed. Secretary Kerry said it best in Vienna: ''Our task is to chart a course out of hell.''

Since the start of the Syrian war, as you outlined, Mr. Chairman, over 225,000 Syrians have died and we face the largest refugee crisis since World War II. The conflict has become a magnet for extremists seeking to change the map of the Middle East, destroy economies and cultures, and terrify an entire population. It is threatening Syria's neighbors Iraq, Jordan, Lebanon, and Turkey, with major consequences for U.S. national interests and beyond.

We are pursuing four interlinked goals. One, to defeat ISIS militarily in both Syria and Iraq. Two, to develop a political transition that gives Syria a future without Bashar al-Assad. Three, to ease the suffering of the Syrian people. And four, to stabilize our allies as they cope with massive refugee outflows.

Our strategy is to leverage military action and intensive diplomacy to achieve a political transition in which Syrians ultimately have a government that respects the rights of its people. This political transition is critical to rooting ISIL out of Syria and ending ISIL's ability to threaten Iraq from Syria.

As Secretary Kerry said in Vienna, ''There is absolutely nothing that could do more to fight Daesh than to achieve a political transition that strengthens the governance capacity of Syria, sideline the person we believe attracts so many foreign fighters and so much terror, and unites the country against terrorism.'' We cannot defeat ISIL in Iraq without also defeating ISIL in Syria.

Moving forward, we first are intensifying the military campaign against ISIL through airstrikes and cooperation with local partners who have already pushed ISIL out of all but 68 miles of the nearly 600-mile border between Syria and Turkey. We and our coalition partners have launched over 2600 strikes in Syria and, thanks to

Turkish support, we are deploying A–10s and F–15s to Incirlik Airbase to expand our strike capacity.

The President, as you mentioned, has ordered the deployment of up to 50 U.S. Special Operations Forces in northern Syria to work with our Arab and Kurdish partners, and we will support them with additional air power.

Next, the United States is providing $150 million a year to the moderate opposition to meet humanitarian needs and provide governance support in areas liberated from ISIL. As the largest single donor since 2011, we have provided over $4.5 billion in humanitarian assistance to Syria. This includes nearly $2.5 billion for aid inside Syria, almost $1 billion for UNHCR programs in Lebanon, and over $650 million to Jordan.

We are enhancing military assistance to help our regional allies, including Jordan and Lebanon, repulse extremist threats from ISIL and Nusra. Thanks to General Allen's leadership, we are leading a global 65-member coalition working to degrade and defeat ISIL.

Mr. Chairman, let me address head-on Russia's dangerous military intervention in Syria. Moscow deployed forces because its ally, the Assad regime, was losing territory, and even Iran support was insufficient to protect it. Moscow has cynically tried to claim that its strikes are focused on terrorists, but, so far, 85 to 90 percent of Syrian strikes have hit the moderate Syrian opposition and they have killed civilians in the process.

Despite our urging, Moscow has yet to stop the Assad regime's horrific practice of barrel-bombing the Syrian people. So, we know that Russia's primary intent is to preserve the regime.

In Vienna, Secretary Kerry brought together all those who can help in the conflict. Iran was invited for the practical reason that it is an active participant that needs to support a political transition. It will come as no surprise to you that this group disagreed on several subjects, most notably, the fate of Assad.

They did agree, however, to convene regime and opposition representatives on the basis of the Geneva Communique of 2012 which set out goals for the transfer of power to a transitional governing body and to explore modalities for a ceasefire in parallel with the political process. They also agree we must preserve Syria's unit and territorial integrity, ensure state institutions remain intact, protect the rights of all Syrians, assure humanitarian access, defeat ISIL and other terrorist groups designated by the U.N. Security Council, and establish a political process leading to a new constitution and elections administered under U.N. supervision and standards. We will convene parties at the ministerial level in the next few weeks to discuss next steps.

Mr. Chairman, no one has any illusions about the difficulty of these efforts, but one thing is clear: Assad cannot unite and govern Syria and we cannot continue to hold the lives of the Syrian people hostage to the desire of one man to remain power. We, the Syrian people, and our regional allies need a political transition that ends ISIL's reign of terror and allows displaced Syrians to return home.

Thank you, Mr. Chairman. I would be happy to take questions.

[The prepared statement of Ambassador Patterson follows:]

Testimony

Before the House Foreign Affairs Committee

U.S. Policy after Russia's Escalation in Syria

Statement of

Ambassador Anne W. Patterson

Assistant Secretary of State for Near Eastern Affairs

November 4, 2015

Chairman Royce, Ranking Member Engel, Members of the Committee, thank you for the opportunity to testify before you and discuss the Administration's policy in Syria, the impact that Russia's recent intervention has had, and our plan for defeating ISIL. Coming on the heels of the President's recent announcement of the Administration's new efforts to intensify the campaign against ISIL and Secretary Kerry's meetings last week in Vienna, where I joined him, chart a path towards a political transition, this hearing is particularly well-timed.

In the four years and a half since the start of the Syrian conflict, when the Asad regime met peaceful protests with violent suppression, over 225,000 Syrians have lost their lives and four million Syrians have become refugees. Approximately half of Syria's pre-war population of 22 million people has been displaced. Many families have been displaced more than five times since the start of the conflict. They are scattered throughout the region and Europe, many losing their possessions, livelihoods, and any hope of returning home.

Since the beginning of Russian strikes in Syria, at least 120,000 Syrians have been displaced as a result of regime offensives aided by Russian airstrikes in the cities of Hama, Aleppo, and Idlib. The conflict in Syria has triggered the world's largest humanitarian crisis since World War II and has become a magnet for violent extremists from around the world. These extremists seek to change the map of the Middle East, to destroy economies and cultures, and to terrify entire populations into submissions to their totalitarian plans.

The security of Syria's neighbors – Iraq, Jordan, Lebanon and Turkey -- is being threatened, with major consequences for U.S. national interests in the region and beyond, including, most importantly, the homeland. Secretary Kerry described the tasks of those gathered in Vienna as "charting a course out of hell." That was not hyperbole.

What We are Doing, and Why

Our interests are undeniable. We have four goals: (1) defeat ISIL militarily in both Syria and Iraq; (2) develop a political transition that gives Syria a future without Bashar al-Asad; (3) ease the suffering of the Syrian people; and, (4) stabilize our regional allies and help European partners as they cope with a massive refugee crisis. Our strategy regarding the Syrian conflict remains fundamentally the same, to leverage military action and diplomacy to achieve a political transition in which Syrians ultimately have a government that respects the rights of its people and Syria retains its unity, independence, territorial integrity and secular character.

This political transition is critical to permanently rooting ISIL out of Syria and ending ISIL's ability to threat Iraq from Syria. As Secretary Kerry said last Friday where I joined him in Vienna, "there is absolutely nothing that could do more to fight ISIL than to a achieve a political transition that strengthens the governance capacity of Syria, sidelines the person that we believe attracts so many foreign fighters and so much terror, and unites the country against terrorism." We cannot defeat ISIL in Iraq without also defeating ISIL in Syria.

Military Initiatives

Let me be clear, the coalition has made progress in our military campaign against ISIL. ISIL has lost significant territory in northern Syria and is now cut off from all but 68 miles of the nearly 600-mile border between Syria and Turkey. We also have reduced the flow of foreign fighters to Syria and are squeezing ISIL's resupply lines.

We are intensifying our campaign against ISIL, both through the airstrikes in Syria and Iraq and by working on the ground with partners in Iraq and Syria who have proven capable of reclaiming territory from ISIL. The United States and our coalition partners have conducted a total of over 7,700 airstrikes against ISIL targets, including 2,600 in Syria. Our coalition is over 65 partners and theirs is three.

As you know, the President has also authorized deployment of up to 50 U.S. Special Operations Forces to northern Syria, where they will help coordinate Arab and Kurdish ground forces. To complement that effort, the Administration has adjusted the Train and Equip program to train vetted groups that are already fighting ISIL on the battlefield, and will support them with additional airpower.

With Turkey's support, we are deploying A-10s and F-15s to Incirlik Airbase to enable the intensification of strikes, and we are increasing our counter-ISIL military assistance to neighboring Jordan and Lebanon. As Secretary of Defense Carter recently testified, U.S. and coalition aircraft will target ISIL with a higher and heavier rate of strikes, including those on ISIL's oil enterprise to weaken its financial resources.

Political Initiatives

To support areas liberated by the moderate opposition, the Administration just announced that the United States will provide nearly $100 million in new assistance to the Syrian opposition, bringing the total to nearly $500 million. This assistance will support local and provincial governance institutions, civil society activists, emergency first responders, and others to meet the increased needs of communities. This is essential as part of the fight against ISIL, but also to the future of Syria after the war; it is essential if Syrians are not forced to flee their towns or the country entirely.

Humanitarian Support

We continue to address the humanitarian consequences of this conflict even as we press to end it. The U.S. is the single largest global donor to the Syrian crisis and has provided over $4.5 billion in critical humanitarian assistance since 2001. Nearly $2.3 billion of this humanitarian assistance is provided inside Syria. An additional $950 million has gone to UNHCR programs in Lebanon and over $650 million to Jordan for refugees and host communities.

<u>Stabilizing Allies</u>

To address the destabilizing effect of the Syrian civil war, we remain committed to helping our close ally Jordan repulse any threats from ISIL or Nusra to Jordanian territory. With Congress' support we have increased our assistance to Jordan, including military equipment and training.

Also with the support of Congress, we also are building up the capabilities of the Lebanese Armed Forces to defend Lebanese territory and the Lebanese people from Daesh, Nusra and other terrorists, despite the risk to Lebanon created by Hizballah's intervention in the Syrian civil war.

Russia's Actions

Mr. Chairman, let me address head-on the issue of Russia's new military deployments and actions in Syria.

Russia intervened in Syria because its ally, the regime of Bashar al-Asad, was losing territory to the opposition. Even direct involvement in combat by Iran, its Hizballah proxies, and Shi'a militia elements from other countries was not enabling the regime to regain territory and protect the areas it considers essential. It's important to remember that Asad took the extraordinary move in June to admit to the public that Syrian forces could not fight throughout the country and the regime could not try to hold all its territory. That was one of the very few times the Asad regime has been truthful with its people.

Russia's military intervention has dangerously exacerbated an already complex environment. As you know, the Asad regime cynically has tried to paint all of those who fight against it as terrorists, so Moscow rationalized its intervention as a fight against ISIL, a rationale Moscow has employed in its intervention, falsely casting its efforts as primarily counter-ISIL. But so far, Russian airstrikes have targeted-predominantly- areas where ISIL is not present. Instead, Russian strikes have targeted the moderate Syria opposition; some of these attacks have killed civilians in strikes on Syrian Civil Defense crews, hospitals, IDP shelters, and ambulances. We have been direct with our Russian counterparts on this point.

So far, then, this has not been a Russian fight against terrorism so much as an effort to preserve the Asad regime. We would have no objection to genuine strikes against ISIL, but Russia can better contribute to the fight against ISIL in Syria by advancing a political transition from Asad. Secretary has engaged them on this and will continue to do this.

Neither we nor the Russians know exactly what effect the Russian action will have over the military balance on the ground – the results so far have been mixed, as the opposition puts up a very strong fight. The conflict and its impact on U.S. interests in the region dictate that we not wait to see that impact before undertaking a full court press to end the war and get to a political settlement. The Russian deployments cannot be used to stiffen the Asad regime's resistance to a political transition. The countries around the table in Vienna – despite their differences – agreed that there is no military solution to the conflict and that there must be a political solution.

Regardless of progress towards a political transition, it is our position that given its new involvement in the military situation, Russia has an even greater responsibility to stop immediately the regime's horrific practice of barrel bombing and use of chlorine gas against its population. The international community looks to Russia to take up that responsibility. The Russian leadership says it has taken up this issue with Asad, but barrel bombing continues almost daily.

Advancing a Political Transition

Mr. Chairman, Ranking Member Engel, last Friday, I joined Secretary Kerry as he brought together in Vienna all those in the region and in Europe who can help end this ever-more-dangerous conflict. Iran was invited for the practical reason that it is an active participant in the Syrian conflict and must help end that conflict through a political settlement.

It will come as no surprise to this Committee that this disparate group did not agree on several subjects – most notably the fate of Asad.

But a group that included the regime's main backers committed to convene the regime and opposition representatives on the basis of the Geneva Communique of 2012 – including the transfer of powers to a transitional governing body.

Despite their differences, these countries did agree on a number of things that need to be done to shape a settlement and Syria's future: preserve Syria's unity, independence, territorial integrity, and pluralistic character; ensure that state institutions will remain intact; protect the rights of all Syrians, regardless of ethnicity or religious denomination; assure humanitarian access throughout the territory of Syria; defeat Da'esh and other terrorist groups as designated by the U.N. Security Council, as well as others agreed by the participants; establish a political process among Syrians leading to credible, inclusive, non-sectarian governance; support the drafting and approval of a new constitution; and hold elections administered under U.N. supervision to international standards. We should not ignore this is an important step.

The participants also agreed to explore modalities for, and implementation of, a nationwide ceasefire to be initiated on a date certain and in parallel with this renewed political process. We are following up on these issues right now, in preparation for reconvening at the ministerial level in the next couple of weeks. Secretary Kerry is committed to pursuing this process as far as it can go.

No one has any illusions about the difficulty of both the diplomatic and the political process among Syrians; our differences with Russia, Iran, and the Asad regime itself are substantial. But one thing is crystal clear and must be accepted by the regime's backers: we cannot continue to make the lives of Syrian people and the security of the region hostage to the desire of one man to retain power. Asad cannot unite and govern Syria; Syrians deserve more. This political process is intended to give them a choice – free from the manipulation, intimidation, and control that the regime has exercised over them for decades.

Extremists have indeed taken advantage of the Syrian people's legitimate struggle against a brutal, power- hungry and corrupt regime. And the extremists must be defeated, because they pose a threat to all of us, including Russia and the West. But make no mistake – this is about ending the rule of regime that has brutalized its people and opened the door to extremism and terrorism throughout the region.

Our diplomatic initiative aims at starting a political process between representatives of Syrians seeking genuine change and the regime – one that the regime will take more seriously than it did the past talks in Geneva. The regime's international backers – Russia and Iran – need to encourage a serious approach to this process. The regime cannot insist, as it now continues to do, that terrorism must be defeated before political change. No one can accept that illogic and such preconditions.

Those of us who support the opposition are already encouraging its representatives to participate in this process seriously, and without preconditions. Deputy Secretary Blinken met a few days ago with Syrian Opposition Coalition President Khaled Khoja, and Special Envoy for Syria Michael Ratney has engaged members of both the external and internal political opposition, the leaders and political representatives of major armed factions, and local governance bodies in Syria to encourage their consolidation around a unified set of principles to guide negotiations and a political transition in Syria that preserves public institutions and the interests of all Syrians.

These groups are coming together around shared ideas and principals more than at any other time during the conflict. We can build on this greater unity to continue to press the regime and its backers to negotiate seriously.

Mr. Chairman, we are now entering a phase of intense diplomacy, even as we increase our strikes against ISIL, continue our support to the moderate opposition, and press the regime to agree to a genuine political transition. As Secretary Kerry reiterated last Friday in Vienna, the choice for Syrians -- and this must be a Syrian-led and Syrian owned process -- must not be between Asad and ISIL. There must be a third option in a transition that moves away from Asad and that can help Syrians -- and all of us -- overcome the extremist challenge.

Thank you and I look forward to responding to your questions.

Chairman ROYCE. Thank you.

We go now to Ambassador Nuland.

STATEMENT OF THE HONORABLE VICTORIA NULAND, ASSIST-ANT SECRETARY, BUREAU OF EUROPEAN AND EURASIAN AFFAIRS, U.S. DEPARTMENT OF STATE

Ambassador NULAND. Thank you, Chairman Royce, members of this committee, for the opportunity to join you and my colleague, Assistant Secretary Anne Patterson today.

While Syria is in Assistant Secretary Patterson's area of responsibility, the conflict there increasingly imperils Turkey, the EU, and the rest of Europe, as refugees stream out of Syria and head both north and south. Russia's new direct combat role in Syria has exacerbated an already-dangerous refugee outflow, straining even the most generous European's ability to cope.

Turkey currently hosts 2.2 million refugees and, by its account, has invested over $8 billion toward their care and well-being. This year the Turkish Coast Guard rescued an estimated 68,000 individuals attempting a dangerous sea voyage.

Just since Russian combat operations began in Syria, Greece has recorded its highest level of migration flows per week with an estimated 48,000 refugees and migrants crossing into the country in 1 week.

The Western Balkans is also stretched thin from increased migration, primarily through Macedonia, Serbia, and Croatia. These countries report an average of 5,000 to 8,000 migrants passing through their borders daily.

Germany is under strain. It has recorded over 577,000 arrivals just in the last 9 months.

Inside Syria, just over the last month while the Russians have been active, the United Nations reports at least 120,000 Syrians have been internally displaced as a result of the regime's attacks aided by Russian airstrikes. Fifty-two thousand eight hundred people were displaced from northern Hama and southern Idlib alone.

These numbers validate what we already know and what you, yourself, Chairman, pointed out. While Moscow asserts that its military actions are directed at ISIL, the vast majority of Russian airstrikes are targeted in areas where the Assad regime has lost territory to forces led by the moderate opposition: Hama, Homs, Aleppo, and Idlib.

Now Russia is fielding its own artillery and other ground assets around Hama and Homs, greatly increasing Russia's own soldiers' vulnerability to counterattack, and Moscow has failed, as you said and as Assistant Secretary Patterson said, to exact any humanitarian concessions from the Assad regime as the price for Russian support. The regime continues to barrel-bomb its own citizens with impunity, perhaps even emboldened by Moscow's help.

None of this has been cost-free for Russia itself. In pure economic terms, the price of its air campaign is estimated at $2 million to $4 million per day, this at a time when average Russians are feeling the pinch of recession brought on by economic mismanagement, low oil prices, and sanctions applied for the Kremlin's last military adventure in Ukraine.

Russian casualties are also reportedly on the rise, although the Kremlin is again working overtime to mask them and silence the loved ones of the lost. As the dumb bombs that Russian is dropping inevitably hit the wrong targets—a market in Damascus, the Aleppo provincial headquarters, and ammunition dump of the Free Syrian Army—Russia is paying a very steep price to its reputation in the fight against terror. That is why, for now, we have limited our own military cooperation with Russia to the most basic of aviation de-confliction procedures to protect our own aircrews.

What would positive cooperation by Russia look like? First, Russia would turn its guns on ISIL and stop the carnage in and around Syria's western cities. As the price of its support, Moscow would insist that Assad ground the helicopters and planes that he is using to barrel-bomb innocents on a daily basis. And it would urgently work with us, our allies, and U.N. Envoy Steffan De Mistura to turn the statement of principles that Secretary Kerry, Foreign Minister Lavrov, and 17 other ministers and institutions released in Vienna last Friday into a true ceasefire, a parallel political transition process, and hasten the day that Assad's bloody tenure comes to an end.

The quality of our cooperation with Russia and Syria depends on the choices that Moscow makes. In the meantime, as the Secretary has said, and as Assistant Secretary Patterson has outlined, we are accelerating the work we are doing to support the moderate Syrian opposition and to protect Syria's neighbors, including those in my area of responsibility, Turkey and the countries of Europe.

Turkey has increased its own participation in the counter-ISIL fight, opening its bases to U.S. and coalition members and conducting its own airstrikes on ISIL targets inside Syria. As we accelerate our own work with Turkey and other like-minded partners to roll back ISIL in northern Syria, a collateral benefit could be the creation of a space where Syrian civilians are free from Assad's barrel bombs as well as ISIL's atrocities.

A large number of Europeans have contributed aviation assets for strike operations in Iraq and some are also considering strike operations in Syria. We are obviously also working with our allies and partners to address the refugee crisis. We have provided Turkey with over $325 million in assistance through the U.N. and private NGOs, and we have provided $26.6 million for UNHCR operations in Europe, including to help with food, water, and legal assistance for refugees, including $600,000 now to respond to requests from Western Balkan countries for equipment and training in the area of border management.

As the Secretary's diplomatic efforts made clear, it is going to take leadership and resolve by dozens of countries and by the Syrians themselves to end the bloodshed there. In Vienna last week, 17 assembled nations, the U.N., and the EU reaffirmed the path forward to peace and a political transition. It remains to be seen whether Russia, Iran, and the Assad regime will join us in walking that path.

We look forward to your questions.

[The prepared statement of Ambassador Nuland follows:]

Testimony Before the House Foreign Affairs Committee
"U.S. Policy after Russia's Escalation in Syria"
Statement of Ambassador Victoria Nuland
Assistant Secretary of State for European and Eurasian Affairs
November 4, 2015

Thank you Chairman Royce, Ranking Member Engel, members of this committee
for the opportunity to join you and my colleague, Assistant Secretary Anne
Patterson today.

While Syria is in Anne's area of responsibility, the conflict there increasingly
imperils Turkey, the EU and the rest of Europe as refugees stream out of Syria and
head both north and south. Russia's new direct combat role in Syria has
exacerbated an already dangerous refugee outflow, straining even the most
generous Europeans' ability to cope.

Turkey currently hosts 2.2 million refugees and by its account, has invested over
$8 billion toward their care and well-being. This year, the Turkish Coast Guard
rescued an estimated 68,000 individuals attempting dangerous sea voyages.

Since Russian combat operations began in Syria, Greece recorded its highest
weekly migration flow of 2015, with approximately 48,000 refugees and migrants
crossing from Turkey into Greece. More than 600,000 individuals have already
entered Greece's maritime borders this year, including 344,953 through the island
of Lesvos, an island of just over 86,400 residents.

On Greece's smaller islands, there have been occasions when the number of daily
arrivals has exceeded the number of registered permanent residents.

The Western Balkans is also stretched thin from increased migration, primarily
through Macedonia, Serbia, and Croatia. These countries report an average of
5,000 to 8,000 migrants passing through their borders daily.

Most of the migrants and refugees are headed north toward Germany, which for
the first 9 months of 2015 recorded 577,000 arrivals.

Inside Syria, just over the last month, the United Nations reports at least 120,000
Syrians have been internally displaced as a result of regime attacks, aided by
Russian airstrikes. In less than two weeks, 52,800 people were displaced in
northern Hama and southern Idlib alone.

These numbers validate what we already know: while Moscow asserts that its military action is directed at ISIL, the vast majority of Russian strikes target areas where the Asad regime has lost territory to forces led by the moderate opposition, in towns like Hama, Homs, Aleppo and Idlib.

Now Russia is fielding its own artillery and other ground assets around Hama and Homs, greatly increasing their soldiers' vulnerability to counterattack. And, Moscow has failed to exact any humanitarian concessions from Asad as the price for Russian support. The regime continues to barrel bomb its own citizens with impunity, perhaps even emboldened by Moscow's help.

None of this has been cost free for Russia. In pure economic terms, the price of its air campaign is estimated at $2-4 million per day. This at a time when average Russians are feeling the pinch of a recession brought on by economic mismanagement, low oil prices, and sanctions applied for the Kremlin's last military adventure: Ukraine.

Russian casualties are also reportedly on the rise, although the Kremlin is again working overtime to mask them and silence the loved ones of the lost. And as the "dumb bombs" Russia is dropping inevitably hit the wrong targets, strikes reported in the media include: a market in Damascus, the Aleppo provincial headquarters, and an ammunition depot of the Free Syrian army.

Russia is paying a steep price to its reputation in the fight against terror.

That is why, for now, we have limited our military cooperation with Russia to the most basic aviation de-confliction to protect our own aircrews. Like our Allies in the international community, we are awaiting further evidence that Russia is sincere in its claims to want to fight ISIL and save Syria for the Syrian people, rather than simply protecting the dictator who bears direct responsibility for the country's destruction.

What would positive cooperation by Russia look like? First, Russia would turn its guns on ISIL and stop the carnage in and around Syria's western cities. As the price of its support, Moscow would insist that Asad ground the helicopters and planes he uses to drop barrel bombs on innocents on a daily basis. And it would urgently work with us, our Allies and UN envoy Steffan De Mistura to turn the statement of principles that Secretary Kerry, FM Lavrov, and 17 other ministers and institutions released in Vienna last Friday into a true ceasefire, and a parallel political transition process that hastens the day that Asad's bloody tenure comes to an end. The quality of our cooperation with Russia in Syria depends on the choices Moscow makes.

In the meantime, as the Secretary has said, we will accelerate the work we are doing to support the moderate Syrian opposition and protect Syria's neighbors including those in my area of responsibility: Turkey and the countries of Europe.

In recent weeks, Turkey has increased its participation in the Counter ISIL Coalition, opening its bases to the U.S. and other Coalition members, and conducting air strikes on ISIL targets inside Syria alongside other Coalition aircraft.

As we accelerate our work with Turkey and other like-minded partners to rollback ISIL in northern Syria, a collateral benefit may be the creation of a space where Syrian civilians are free from Asad's barrel bombs as well as ISIL's atrocities.

A large number of Europeans have contributed aviation assets for strike operations in Iraq and are considering strike operations in Syria.

Belgium, Germany, Italy, The Netherlands, Turkey, and the UK are active co-chairs of Coalition Working Groups with the United States. The Dutch are co-leading on efforts to halt foreign fighter flows, along with many other members of the coalition, and the Italians are co-leading the effort to counter ISIL financing. At home, our EU partners are contributing by: strengthening their counterterrorism laws and intelligence-sharing capabilities; stopping foreign fighters; addressing radicalism; de-legitimizing ISIL ideology; reporting suspicious financial activities in European institutions; and, working with the U.S. to identify and act against ISIL financiers and recruiters.

We are also working with allies and partners to address the refugee crisis. We have provided Turkey with $325 million in assistance, through UN organizations and NGOs, to support the operation of over 100 schools, provide shelter, essential household supplies, mobile registration centers, medical centers, safe spaces for children to learn and play, and cash assistance for vulnerable families.

We have also provided $26.6 million to UNHCR for Europe programs, including for food, water, and legal assistance to refugees transiting Greece, Macedonia, and Serbia, among others; we have supplied grants, humanitarian commodities and donations of excess property and equipment totaling $1.2 million to enhance the humanitarian response in Croatia, Macedonia, Serbia and Turkey; and, we have contributed $600,000 to respond to Western Balkan requests for additional equipment and training in the area of border management.

As the Secretary's diplomatic efforts make clear, it will take leadership and resolve by dozens of countries and the Syrians themselves to end the bloodshed there. In Vienna last week, 17 assembled nations, the UN and EU reaffirmed the path forward to peace and a political transition. It remains to be seen whether Russia, Iran and the Asad regime will join us in walking it.

I look forward to your questions.

———

Chairman ROYCE. Thank you, Ambassador Nuland.

I mentioned my frustration with how the administration has approached Syria and ISIS. The fact is that we had the State Department here, officials, in front of this committee 2 years ago sounding the ISIS alarm, explaining that action had to be taken.

The Iraqis and our own officials pushed for airstrikes early on and pushed for those airstrikes when ISIS was most vulnerable in Raqqa, in Syria, but the White House sat paralyzed. Once the airstrikes did start—and that is after a year of watching cities fall from Fallujah to Mosul and the Central Bank being taken over by ISIS—after that, we finally saw airstrikes averaging 19 a day, but in a circumstance in which three-quarters, because of exceedingly restrictive rules of engagement, three-quarters of those planes flew back to their bases without dropping their ordnance. If we compare that and consider the first Gulf War, Desert Storm, those airstrikes averaged 1,000 combat sorties per day, not 19.

And now, enter the Russians. The State Department said that this wouldn't impact our air mission over Syria. And yet, the numbers that the committee put together say otherwise. In October, while the Russians did 800 airstrikes for the full month, mostly aimed, by the way, at the opposition, we managed just 100 against ISIS.

Assistant Secretary Patterson, are we ceding the skies to Russia here and, in effect, allowing the ISIS threat to grow, because, after all, ISIS has gained territory here during this timeframe? So say the NGOs on the ground.

Ambassador PATTERSON. Mr. Chairman, obviously, I am not from DoD, but let me try to answer this question. Actually, this question came up at a very high-level meeting, and I will quote to you what a senior military officer said, which is we don't hit targets we can't see—and this was in reference to the very bad weather that had overtaken the area last week when the strikes were limited—and that we can't be compared to the Russians in any moral or operation or tactical sense.

The battlefield, I might suggest, Mr. Chairman, is very different and a very complex battlefield mixed in with civilians. There are very high standards vis-à-vis collateral damage and civilian casualties that I would suggest the Russian air force is not subject to, and that we are appropriately subject to, which is different, very different, than the first Gulf War and the amass of conventional forces.

So, that I think is at least a partial answer, Mr. Chairman, to your question.

Chairman ROYCE. Well, from the way I perceive it here, especially given my frustration with the first year of this conflict and not utilizing any air power when it could be very effective, we have a situation today where we are hitting the bad guys in this, ISIS, 100 times, and the Russians are hitting those that are opposed to ISIS and Assad 800 times. That is my takeaway in a broad sense of where we are now.

But, Ambassador Nuland, this isn't just Russia reaching out to save an old ally, when we look at those remarks. We are seeing Russia and Iran work together in ways most had not expected. I certainly don't think the administration expected it. I don't think they expected we find Hezbollah fighters and Iranian Quds Forces and Russian headquarters working together in this kind of a circumstance.

But this was General Soleimani traveling to Moscow in the middle of our nuclear negotiations and putting this plan in place. Twice, as I understand it, he made that travel, in violation, by the way, of the embargo. Again, something that wasn't objected to when I raised the issue that the head of the Quds Forces, who by the way was responsible himself indirectly for the death of some 600 Americans, I am told by the Pentagon, that he was in Moscow making arrangements with the Russians. There was no protest that I am aware of, of this being a violation of the travel ban.

Of late, Russian aircraft have been seen running Iranian weapons into Syria. Again, that is a very clear violation of the embargo which we all support.

So, what steps are being taken to uphold the U.N. arms embargo on Iran in the face of the Russian violations?

Ambassador PATTERSON. Mr. Chairman, I am unaware of those reports about the movement of Iranian arms into Syria on Russian aircraft, but we will certainly get you a report as soon as possible.

Chairman ROYCE. Thank you.

I am out of time. I will mention, when Mr. Engel returns—he is at the White House—we will give him ample time for his opening statement and for his questions.

But, in the meantime, I think Karen Bass of California is next in the queue.

Ms. BASS. Thank you, Mr. Chair.

In light of the President's statement last week that we were deploying 50 Special Operation Forces to Syria, I wanted to know what you see as their mission. Do you expect them to be engaged in direct combat? And how can we be sure that this limited deployment won't be a slippery slope to involve U.S. troops?

I would join my colleague, Ms. Frankel, who said that, had we not invaded Iraq years ago, that the whole region wouldn't be destabilized as it is now. But, in light of that, I wanted to know if you could respond.

I also want to ask you a couple of questions regarding a future transitional government in Syria.

Ambassador PATTERSON. Thank you.

Let me say that I was in a briefing yesterday, and some of these responses on the activities and location of the Special Forces are classified.

Ms. BASS. Sure.

Ambassador PATTERSON. And so, perhaps we will come back to you in a written answer on that.

Ms. BASS. Okay.

Ambassador PATTERSON. We would be very happy to do so. And their exact role is also a classified response.

But let me also say that we are also deploying, as I mentioned in my statement, additional aircraft to Incirlik. The President is looking at a number of other options to intensify our efforts in this battle space.

Ms. BASS. In terms of the future transitional government in Syria, there were talks held in Vienna last week, and I wanted to know if you could talk about those. In the future, what do you feel is the best way to compel the regime to a negotiated transition? And that is for either one of you.

Ambassador PATTERSON. Yes. Let me give you an outline, if I might, a brief one, of the Secretary's conversations in Vienna last week.

He brought together 20 countries, including the Russians and the Iranians and our Gulf allies and the Turks, to discuss a way forward. We agreed, obviously, to disagree on the future of Assad, but he did plot a way forward on a transitional government/constitutional reform, and a series of meetings and working groups that would take place with the international community, with the U.N., and with the opposition to try to implement the Geneva Communique of 2012.

The next meeting will likely be in Vienna within the next 2 weeks. There will be a series of groups and consultations with the U.N. beforehand and with the opposition. The idea is to have a transitional government, to work on a timetable for Assad's departure—and let me be clear that that is a critical element of this policy—and, then, to work on constitutional review and, ultimately, an election in Syria. That is the basic outlines of Secretary Kerry's strategy.

Ms. BASS. So, at this point, if there were to be a transitional government, who do you see composing that?

Ambassador PATTERSON. Well, a number of opposition figures and people already on the ground. It would be key—and this was in the Communique—that Syria's institutions, the military, intelligence, police, civil service, would remain intact. So, you wouldn't have a total collapse of state authority. The idea is just to remove Bashar al-Assad——

Ms. BASS. Like what happened in Iraq?

Ambassador PATTERSON [continuing]. And his cronies from power.

Ms. BASS. Thank you. I yield back my time.

Mr. CONNOLLY. Would my colleague yield?

Ms. BASS. Oh, yes, sure.

Mr. CONNOLLY. Ambassador Nuland, what in the world makes us think Russia would agree to that? Why would Russia agree to a transitional government with opposition figures and the removal of Assad? And did you get that commitment?

Ambassador NULAND. Congressman, Russia did agree to that general framework in 2012 when it signed onto the original——

Mr. CONNOLLY. Well, that is before they started bombing and military activities on the ground. It is now 2015. You had a meeting in Vienna. Did the Russians agree?

Ambassador NULAND. So, as Assistant Secretary Patterson has said, they have agreed to the general framework that we need a ceasefire, we need a transitional government, we need elections. The area of dispute is at what stage in that process Assad departs the scene.

Mr. CONNOLLY. Well, I must say my time is up, but given what is happening on the ground, that sounds like fantasy to me.

Chairman ROYCE. Mr. Chris Smith of New Jersey.

Mr. SMITH. Thank you very much. Thank you, Mr. Chairman for calling this important hearing.

Welcome to our two distinguished witnesses.

Let me just ask a couple of questions. First, I chaired a hearing last week with the Helsinki Commission on refugees emanating or coming out of Syria, and the High Commissioner's Regional Representative testified. His bottom line was that there were two big trends that have led to the mass exodus. One, a political solution will not be found anytime soon to the war. Secondly, after so many years in exile, many people's resources have dwindled to next to nothing.

But he said the third factor is the trigger. It is the raison d'etre why people have up-staked and have made their way into Europe. He said the trigger was that a few months ago there was a lack of funding for the World Food Programme. They cut their assistance by 30 percent. And he testified and said, as a consequence, many refugees felt that the international community could be starting to abandon them.

He pointed out as well that the interagency Syria Regional Refugee and Resilience plan for 2015 is only 41 percent funded. People are living on less than 50 cents a day. He said they decided to go into flight.

My question would be, I know we are generous supporters of the WFP and I am very glad that Congress and the administration has done that. But did we anticipate that this might be a trigger, that there was such a huge cut to the World Food Programme?

Secondly, let me ask, as Iran reaps its billions of dollars in windfall attributed to the Iranian nuclear deal, what is your assessment? Of course, you could provide this in a written form to elaborate on it. But what is your assessment of how that cash might be used to assist Assad?

I also asked Assistant Secretary Richard last week about establishing a P–2 program for especially minorities like the Yazidis and the Christians who really don't pose a threat. I know we have a very, very robust vetting process, as we ought to, to ensure that we don't have ISIS or any other al-Qaeda types embedded in the refugees that come here. But a P–2 that targets people who are far less likely to be a threat to Americans seems to be something that I hope is on the table being very actively discussed.

I yield.

Ambassador PATTERSON. Mr. Smith, let me go through those as quickly as possible. On the question of the reduction in WFP, let me first say that we have done everything humanly possible to increase our contribution to WFP and to also solicit contributions from some or our prosperous allies in the Gulf who, in truth, have come through with an enormous amount of money, up to $2 billion for the Syrian refugees.

Mr. SMITH. Pardon my interruption. But is that getting to the people, so they know?

Ambassador PATTERSON. Did we anticipate that it would be a trigger? I can't answer that, but we certainly anticipated that it would be a huge problem and deprive these people of desperately-needed resources. So, we are doing everything we can to beef up our humanitarian support.

On the question of Iranian resources, I know this has been a frequent discussion with this committee and with other committees. The Iranian economy has been in free fall for the past several years because of sanctions. We believe there are huge pent-up needs in infrastructure, energy, reconstruction, consumer demand that the Iranian Government will have to meet and Rouhani, in particular, as an elected leader, will have to meet. But I don't want to be naive, Mr. Smith, that some of this money won't be used for the destabilizing activities of General Qasem Soleimani.

Then, finally, I know that you had asked my colleague Anne Richard that, about P–2 program. Let me say, of course, that there is, frankly, a lot of concern, Mr. Smith, about people coming out of this area, that they are properly vetted and reviewed, given some of the history. But I know you have asked that and, believe me, it will certainly be under consideration, and we will get you a staffed-out answer.

Chairman ROYCE. Mr. Bill Keating of Massachusetts.

Mr. KEATING. Thank you, Mr. Chairman.

I realize you are not speaking for the Department of Defense, as Assistant Secretary Patterson had mentioned. However, I just want to ask you if you have been at briefings and things you could disclose. Because in open hearings with this committee and subcommittees, we have had witnesses, generals, military experts, time after time saying that the unilateral approach of just bombing itself would not be effective strategy, that it had to be accompanied by the ability with troops on the ground to hold that area they had bombed. Otherwise, it was basically a worthless military strategy and approach.

And so, it brings me back to my opening comments where I said simply bombing by itself without the ability, whether it be through Sunni Arab troops or other troops on the ground, or in absentia U.S. troops, the criticism about not continuing on that bombing aspect, it has to be incorporated with a land force complement.

So, are you familiar with those kinds of discussions, Assistant Secretary?

Ambassador PATTERSON. Yes, Mr. Keating, those topics, as you suggest, are frequently discussed within the administration. And let me first say that I think the bombing campaign has had very considerable impact on the leadership of ISIL. I can get you the exact figures, but a number of prominent leaders have been essentially taken off the battlefield and removed from office.

Mr. KEATING. Can I just jump in? Thank you. Can I just jump into this aspect? There has been a lot of discussion about rules of engagement, and it is a very difficult issue. But Russia is approaching this in a manner where, without discrimination, they seem contented bombing and killing innocent civilians, and not even trying to make efforts to avoid doing that, as opposed to the U.S. policy which takes that into consideration, as most countries in the world do. Can you comment on the importance of following rules of engagement to try, as the U.S. does, to minimize civilian deaths?

Ambassador PATTERSON. Yes, Mr. Keating. As I mentioned, we have, particularly in this campaign, we have very strict, the U.S. Air Force has very strict rules of engagement on collateral damage, and that is in accordance with the President's instructions that our job is to minimize civilian casualties in every way possible.

It is not only, might I mention, Mr. Keating, a moral issue, but it is also an issue of practicality, that you don't want to alienate, that the United States does not want to alienate the people on the ground.

If I might go back to your issue of the ground forces, let me also say that one of our goals now is to work with partners on the ground who can serve this role as ground troops in support of a U.S. air campaign. We have supported, as you know, the Syrian Kurds and the Syrian Arabs, the Syrian Arab Coalition, and it has been very effective, I think, in closing the border, both to the influx of foreign fighters and to the export of refined products that provide revenue for ISIL.

Mr. KEATING. Is it fair to say, is it a fair statement to say that, not to categorize the Russian bombing actions as decisive, but rather immoral? Is that a fair statement?

Ambassador PATTERSON. Yes, I would say that. I read yesterday rather graphic reports of the civilian casualties that they had inflicted on a village nearby. It seems quite indiscriminate, if I might say so.

Mr. KEATING. Okay. Thank you. I yield back.

Chairman ROYCE. Thank you, Mr. Keating.

We go to Mr. Jeff Duncan of South Carolina.

Mr. DUNCAN. Thank you, Mr. Chairman. Thanks for holding this hearing.

We are seeing a tremendous migration crisis in Europe as a result of the Syrian civil war and ISIS aggression in western Iraq and in Syria. This migration crisis is really threatening regional stability in Europe really to the tune that we hadn't seen since probably the 1930s. It is mind-boggling when you watch the videos of the number of migrants streaming into Eastern European countries and now Western European countries.

I just have a question for Ambassador Nuland. Ambassador Colleen Bell works for you, does she not? Okay. The Ambassador to Hungary for the record.

Ambassador NULAND. Yes.

Mr. DUNCAN. You were also Ambassador to NATO. So, you understand the key role that NATO countries play with the security of the world and with cooperating with the United States, correct? Hungary is a very valuable ally, NATO ally, are they not?

Ambassador NULAND. Yes.

Mr. DUNCAN. So, why, then, after months of seemingly improved relations between Hungary, a western democracy and a NATO ally, as we have just confirmed, did the U.S. Ambassador decide to launch an unprovoked attack on Hungary last week? You are familiar with what Ms. Bell said, correct?

Ambassador NULAND. Congressman, I am not sure specifically what comments of hers you may be referring to. She gave a speech last week where she reaffirmed U.S. support for a Hungary that is increasingly democratic. We have had concerns about government policy with regard to attacking corruption. We have had concerns about repression of media. I think she was probably, if it is the speech on——

Mr. DUNCAN. She chastised the sovereign nation's ability to secure its own borders and put fencing up, if they so chose, did she not?

Ambassador NULAND. Again, I would have to go back and look at precisely what she said. We have had concerns, as has the EU as a whole, about EU member states erecting fences, against EU policy, between each other. We have, instead, tried to support the policy of the EU as a whole to work together and to be in solidarity with each other in addressing the migrant crisis by registering, by——

——

Mr. DUNCAN. I mean, I disagree. I disagree with some of that, based on what she said. So, the question to you is, is our diplomatic mission not to improve relations with our allies or is it one to scold those we need in NATO in order to meddle in their domestic affairs while stroking whatever egos are satisfied by such actions? Is that our diplomatic mission there?

Ambassador NULAND. Congressman, even with our NATO allies, it has been the longstanding, one might argue 50-year, policy of the United States to support an increasingly democratic, stable, clean Europe. So, when we have concerns that a country is not attacking corruption in its midst, when we have concerns about the rollback of the democratic principles that undergird NATO membership, we are going to speak out about it, yes.

Mr. DUNCAN. Well, Madam Ambassador, I disagree. I do think you are meddling in the affairs of a sovereign nation. When we look at the mass migration that is coming across Europe, are you going to interfere and chastise Germany if they decide to deal with the migrants that are affecting their nation? Are you going to chastise Slovenia or some of the other nations who are having to deal with this? They are having to deal with these huge—almost 1 million migrants have made their way into Eastern and now Western Europe. It is an issue, a crisis for them. The demographic is going to change the political atmosphere in those countries. These are sovereign nations that are going to have to deal with this. It is going to be a strain on their social programs, on their ability to do things for their own citizens. The demands being placed on them by these migrants, it is a game-changer in Europe.

Is the U.S. policy one to interfere with sovereign nations in Europe and their ability to provide services for their own citizens and deal with the migration crisis? Is that the policy of the administration?

Ambassador NULAND. On the contrary, Congressman, we are strongly supportive of the overall EU policy that they are putting in place now, which is to support each other in resettling these migrants appropriately and treating them tolerantly and sharing the burden in contributing to post-country—in providing more funds to those countries where refugees are coming from.

Mr. DUNCAN. My time is just about up, Madam Ambassador.

Ambassador NULAND. However, when they start rebuilding walls between themselves and among themselves in contradiction of EU policy, we are going to support those who support——

Mr. DUNCAN. I would recommend that you listen to Ms. Bell's statements and we have a retraction on that.

I yield back.

Chairman ROYCE. We go now to Lois Frankel of Florida.

Ms. FRANKEL. Thank you.

Well, first, I thank you for being here. I think you are just hearing some frustration. You know not to take this personally from anyone. But thank you.

First of all, I just want to say and applaud, I think, the administration, the President, Mr. Kerry trying to get as many of the relevant world leaders together to try to come to grips with what is going on in Syria, is going in the right direction. That is a good step.

It sounds to me that you, from comments especially—I forget which one of you said this—but it sounds to me that it is your opinion that Russia's actions in Syria are such that it will be self-destructive. I think that is what I glean from your comments.

But, in the meantime, before Russia self-destructs themselves with what they are doing, there are so many innocent people who are being harmed. So, my question is, what kind of strategies or actions are you taking with Russia that can maybe change their course? That is my first question.

Second is, what are we doing to actually protect the Syrian civilians within Syria and are there any further plans or is it hopeless to do a safe zone or a no-fly zone? Or is anything else being considered that we have not heard about?

Ambassador PATTERSON. Ms. Frankel, let me say, first, that we don't think this is a slam dunk from the Russians by any means. They have basically got the whole Sunni world against them now, and I think it is an analytical fact that we may not have seen anything yet in terms of Jihad, because we have already seen imams in the Gulf call for increased Jihad against the godless Russian presence in Syria. So, I won't say they have bitten off more than they can chew, but they certainly have issues that they are going to confront, not the least of which is their huge Islamic population inside and on the perimeter of Russia vis-à-vis the civilians inside Syria, Ms. Frankel.

Of course, half the assistance is provided, our humanitarian assistance to the tunes of billions of dollars provided to Syrians within Syria. Of course, there are zones we can't reach. But in terms of safe zones—and I am glad you asked this because there has been a lot of discussion about this—this is a hugely-complex and resource-intensive issue.

And the administration has looked at this over and over and over again, and there is no option on the table, nor recommended by the Department of Defense, that does not require a massive amount of air support would, then, detract from the effort against ISIL. We continue to look at this. We continue to study this, but there is no viable option on the table at this time.

Ms. FRANKEL. Ambassador Nuland, did you have anything to add?

Ambassador NULAND. Simply to say that we have been very clear with the Russians about what we are seeing in terms of the results of their strikes. The Secretary has spoken to Foreign Minister Lavrov virtually every day; also, about our insistence that they exact some kind of restraint out of Assad for the support that they are giving, at least in the area of barrel-bombing. We will continue to share not only with the Russians directly, but with all of you and publicly, what we see. I think, as Assistant Secretary Patterson said, what the Secretary's hope is here is that, if you rope them into this diplomacy, they will see a better way to a peaceful solution than what they are doing.

Ms. FRANKEL. Just one more question. I think we all have heard that the conditions for these Syrian refugees are dire, especially at the borders. I heard stories yesterday that my hair would go up straight if it could do that, but it sounded horrible.

What kind of actions are you taking? I mean, I heard people living out in the open, no sanitation, very little food. What is the response?

Ambassador PATTERSON. Ms. Frankel, occasionally, the neighboring countries close the border and these poor people get caught in these pockets. Usually, that is short-lived and the countries will open the border again. And so, we work with them constantly on that issue, to get these refugees into their countries.

Most of these countries are hosting these refugees in host communities, and it puts a very significant strain on their public services and education, which is why support from the international community and continued financial support is so important.

Ms. FRANKEL. Thank you.

Thank you, Mr. Chair.

Chairman ROYCE. Thank you. Thank you, Ms. Frankel.

Okay. Mr. Darrell Issa of California.

Mr. ISSA. Thank you, Mr. Chairman, Ambassador, Ambassador.

Subject du jour, Syria. Fourteen years ago, I made my first trip to Syria to meet with the unknown President Assad. He has been pretty well-defined over 14 years, and the Alawite dictatorship he heads has been pretty well defined over many decades.

So, let me ask a question and, Ambassador Patterson, I think I will primarily frame it to you. More than 4 years, this administration called for regime change and not only did very little to make that come about, but, then, directly and through the Russians, negotiated various agreements, including, obviously, the chemical weapons departure.

At this point, isn't it time to ask the question of, what do we really want to achieve in Syria since, one, the so-called Free Syrian Army has cost us some incredible number that I am not even going to say on television again, because it has been a complete failure. We have no Free Syrian Army. More Sunnis are fighting independent of us than with us by a factor of probably 1,000 to 1.

So, let me ask you it in succinct way. Ambassador, isn't it time we figure out what is possible in a Syria that allows the millions of Syrians, Sunni, Shia, Alawite, Christian to return to their country?

Ambassador PATTERSON. Mr. Issa, we don't believe it is possible to have any sort of settlement there, either a political settlement or any military defeat of ISIL, without the departure of Assad. These two issues now are inexorably linked. He has turned out to be, as you know, a magnet for terrorists all over the world, particularly, well, for many countries, even including our own.

I guess I would differ from you that the Free Syrian Army has been a bust. I think there are efforts underway that, if corralled—

and I know that you are aware of these efforts underway that have corralled our Gulf allies and our European allies in a common effort in Syria. So, I think there is really no alternative but to talk about his departure.

Mr. ISSA. Ambassador, I am not for a moment trying to predetermine the departure of Bashar al-Assad. I happen to agree with you that a future Syria should be a Syria with greater Sunni representation, with rights of Christians respected, and that he is probably not the ideal—he is a failed leader in many ways and I think history has already borne that out.

But my question, and the reason I am asking it this way, is, if I were to ask you, do we have an effective battalion of Free Syrian military, you would have to say no. If I said, do we have an effective company, you would have to say no. If I asked if we had an effective platoon, you would say, well, we have got a platoon, but it is not quite effective.

I just left the Marines' 240th birthday. Trust me, if I sent Marines in to evaluate those people, they would come up short of effective for any of them, and it has been 4 years.

Isn't it true that the effective forces against Assad today are, in fact, non-ISIS fighters who disagree, but are not aligned with us; in other words, Sunnis who oppose Assad who are being bombed by the Russians as we speak?

Ambassador PATTERSON. That is true in the north, Mr. Issa. I would say that it is not true in the south. But, certainly, in the north, the al-Nusra Front, which is an al-Qaeda affiliate, has absorbed, as have other smaller groups, have absorbed a number of what we would have previously called the moderate opposition, yes, that is correct. It is not true in the south, Mr. Issa, where I believe the moderate fighters are holding their own and holding territory.

Mr. ISSA. And let's go to the moderate fighters in the south and the effect on Lebanon for just a moment, which is the lead question people always assume I will ask. Today in Lebanon it has been widely reported, unclassified, that, in fact, the sectors that are being protected in Lebanon from ISIS are, in fact, a combination of the Lebanese armed forces, wherever possible, and Hezbollah in many of the Shia areas essentially protecting their own.

Is that a workable solution and is the United States able to ensure that the Lebanese armed forces continue to get what they need will not unreasonably embolden Hezbollah for the future?

Ambassador PATTERSON. Mr. Issa, I think the Lebanese armed forces under the circumstances have done nothing short of a remarkable job in protecting Lebanon. We have tried to increase the flow of material to them. We have, as you know, a robust training program by some of our highly-trained American forces. We have worked particularly with the Saudis to get them some additional funds to buy military equipment. It is an extremely high priority. I think they just had an encounter with ISIL day before yesterday. Contrary to many expectations, it seems to be working.

Mr. ISSA. And I want to thank you, Mr. Chairman, for this opportunity on Syria, and I want to thank the Ambassador for pointing out the success, which is Lebanon hosting nearly a third of its population as refugees while keeping ISIS out of that country. Thank you.

Chairman ROYCE. Thank you, Mr. Issa, for making that point.

Joaquin Castro of Texas.

Mr. CASTRO. Thank you, Chairman, and thank you, Ambassadors, for being here today, for your testimony, and, most of all, for your service to the country.

My first question is on migration. What effect has the Russian bombing campaign had on the flow of migrants, whether it has changed it, whether it has increased it? What is our read on that?

Ambassador NULAND. Congressman Castro, as I said in my opening, we believe that it has led to an acceleration of migrants into Europe, in particular. We have seen those upticks in Greece, in Turkey, into Germany just since the Russian bombing.

Mr. CASTRO. And have we found that the migrants intend to stay in Europe or want to come back? What is our understanding of that?

Ambassador NULAND. With regard to Syrians, what we are getting from our European friends is that it is a mixed picture. You know, those who have hope that their country can come back together have left some relatives there and property, but many of them have lost hope and are looking for permanent resettlement in Europe, which is a question that Europe is struggling with.

Mr. CASTRO. Sure. What about our Gulf partners? What role have they played with respect to migration and refugees?

Ambassador PATTERSON. Our Gulf partners have been generous with funding. The Kuwaitis, in particular, have hosted three funding donors' conferences, given hundreds of millions of dollars, the United Arab Emirates as well.

Perhaps the question you are asking is on the resettlement. The Gulf countries do not take in refugees. What they do is take in, basically, guest workers, and a number of the Gulf countries have a large number of Syrian employees really, but you cannot say that they are refugees. But they have been generous with their money.

Mr. CASTRO. My second question is on the use of chemical weapons. Of course, in 2013, Russia agreed to essentially extract the chemical weapons from Syria, and Syria is now bound by the Chemical Weapons Convention. What kind of use of chemical weapons have we seen in Syria, specifically with regard to chlorine gas?

Ambassador PATTERSON. We believe that we have seen chlorine gas. It would be a violation of the Chemical Weapons Convention, of which, of course, Syria is a signatory. We have referred it to the Organization for Prohibition of Chemical Weapons, and they are going to do an analysis and a report. Once we receive that, we will decide what steps to take.

Mr. CASTRO. Have we determined that it is the Assad regime that is using the chemical weapons or could it be other actors as well?

Ambassador PATTERSON. Our strong judgment is it is the Assad regime because they were seemingly dropped from helicopters, which are not in the possession of the opposition.

Mr. CASTRO. Thank you. I yield back, Chairman.

Chairman ROYCE. Thank you, Mr. Castro.

Now we go to Mr. Mo Brooks of Alabama.

Mr. BROOKS. Thank you, Mr. Chairman.

In your opinion, is Russia's use of military force in Syria good or bad, productive or counterproductive?

Ambassador NULAND. Congressman Brooks, I think we have been pretty clear here that we do not think that Russia's military intervention is leading to a settlement of the Syrian conflict, that, instead, it is giving Assad confidence that he can stay in power.

Mr. BROOKS. Using words such as ''immoral'' to describe how bad Russia's conduct in Syria, is that fair?

Ambassador NULAND. Assistant Secretary Patterson confirms that word and I don't have a problem with it, either.

Mr. BROOKS. What thought has been given to using a diversion strategy whereby we force the Russian military to be engaged in different parts of the globe; thereby, weakening their abilities to prosecute their military aggression in Syria? More specifically, how would a more aggressive military action in the Ukraine impact Russia's limited ability to expand its military operations in the Middle East? And by ''military action,'' I am talking about where we arm the Ukrainians; thereby, forcing the Russians to divert some of their military capabilities from Syria and other parts of the globe to Ukraine to try to protect the territory that they have either unlawfully invaded themselves or assisted their proxies in unlawfully invading.

Ambassador NULAND. Congressman, I think you know that we have had a ceasefire in Ukraine that has largely been holding, not completely, but largely been holding since September 1st. I am confident that you would not be suggesting here that the Ukrainians reignite the war to draw the Russians deeper into conflict there. I don't think that would be good for Ukraine or for the stability of Europe.

Mr. BROOKS. Well, is this ceasefire, in actuality, just a way in which the Russians and their proxies can consolidate their territorial gains? Is that putting Ukraine in a position where they have to forfeit hopes of recapturing the land wrongfully taken by Russia and its proxies?

Ambassador NULAND. Congressman, under the Minsk Agreement, as you know, the first step is ceasefire; the second step is pull back of weapons, then political progress in the Donbass, and then, return of the territory and closure of the border. So, what we are now starting to see for the first time in the 2 years of this conflict is some pullback of Russian and separatists' weapons. So, that is a good thing. We are seeing that in Luhansk and now we are starting to see that in Donetsk, even though the ceasefire is not complete and we have had some tactical attacks in the last couple of days.

So, again, if you want Ukraine to get that territory back, if you want Minsk implemented, what is most important is to lean on Russia and the separatists to complete those obligations, pull back their weapons, and allow real elections and allow return of the border.

Mr. BROOKS. Well, as of today, given the shifting of military equipment, has any of the territory taken by Russia or its proxies been returned to the Government of the Ukraine, any significant amount of territory? And if you could, if you are going to be able to answer that, give us all an idea as to how much, what percentage of territory has been returned to the Ukraine after Russia's invasion and how much has been kept in the hands of the Russians, keeping in mind that the Crimea itself is a rather large land mass.

Ambassador NULAND. About 7 percent of Ukraine, if you count Crimea plus the occupation of eastern Ukraine, is lost to the control of the Ukrainian Government. As I said, with this ceasefire and the beginning of pullback of heavy weapons, Ukrainian authorities have not had access to that territory, but, increasingly, OSCE monitors have had access, and we need to encourage and accelerate that process. If we can get to——

Mr. BROOKS. One second. So, is your answer to the question zero?

Ambassador NULAND. Zero.

Mr. BROOKS. As of today, zero land has been returned to the Ukrainian Government?

Ambassador NULAND. As of today, zero.

Mr. BROOKS. How much in the way of weapons has the United States delivered to the Ukrainian Government in order to enhance Ukraine's ability to defend its territory?

Ambassador NULAND. Congressman, through bipartisan generosity of both halves of this Congress, we have supplied over $266 million in security support for Ukraine. That includes extensive training of the national guard, now moving on to training the military. We have provided lots of kinds of non-lethal assistance, including UAVs——

Mr. BROOKS. Okay. I am talking about weaponry. What weaponry has been given to the Ukrainian Government to enable it to defend its territory or to recapture territory taken by Russia?

Ambassador NULAND. It depends how you define weaponry, but we have provided counter-radar batteries, including short-range and now longer-range ones——

Mr. BROOKS. Any missiles?

Ambassador NULAND [continuing]. UAVs. We have not provided lethal assistance to date.

Mr. BROOKS. No tanks?

Ambassador NULAND. No, but we have provided combat vehicles like humvees, night vision, combat protection, et cetera.

Mr. BROOKS. Mr. Chairman, with indulgence, may I have 30 more seconds?

Chairman ROYCE. Yes, Mr. Brooks.

Mr. BROOKS. Thank you.

The reason I mention this is due to the leadership of Congressman Engel, who is not here at the moment, of New York, the House passed a resolution in March of this year by a 348-to-48 vote, about an 88-percent-to-12-percent bipartisan vote, which is overwhelming in the United States House of Representatives and to some degree a little bit unusual.

That resolution of the House of Representatives in an overwhelming bipartisan fashion stated,

"That the House of Representatives strongly urges the President to fully and immediately exercise the authorities provided by Congress to provide Ukraine with lethal defensive weapon systems to enhance the ability of the people of Ukraine to defend their sovereign territory from the unprovoked and continuing aggression of the Russian Federation.''

I would hope that you would carry back to this administration that message with a double benefit. One is we help Ukraine fight against aggression and, two, I would submit that it weakens Russia and Syria, which, in turn, helps to alleviate some of the problems that we have there.

Thank you for your indulgence.

Chairman ROYCE. Thank you, Mr. Brooks.

Robin Kelly of Illinois.

Ms. KELLY. Thank you, Mr. Chair.

About 10,000 ISIS fighters have been killed this past year, but it seems like, despite that, they have been replaced by new recruits, new fighters. If we are going to destroy them, how do we cut off those new fighters, those new recruits?

Ambassador PATTERSON. That is a big challenge, Congressman, and let me tell you the steps that are being taken. First, there is a step, under General Allen's leadership, who regrettably he is soon to leave the position. We have developed a number of working groups with our allies, for instance, with the United Arab Emirates, to try to message, to try to get to these young men and persuade them that ISIL isn't a viable future.

We have worked with the Turkish Government—Ambassador Nuland can speak more to that—to close the border. And again, most of the border now is closed. We have worked with them to deport individuals who try to cross over into Turkey, into Syria.

We have worked with our Gulf allies, again, to increase their message and their surveillance of individuals who might undertake extremist activities in Syria.

But it is a big challenge, Congresswoman, because ISIL has managed to tap into Sunni grievances in a very big way. But we continue to press on this. I believe we are having some modest success, but, obviously, that is key to restraining the growth of ISIL.

Ms. KELLY. What do you think about even the Americans going over? Have we had success in decrease those amounts?

Ambassador PATTERSON. I think, all told, Congresswoman, there are really just a handful of Americans. I think, frankly, our law enforcement agencies and the communities that they work with, I think that is the key in the United States, is to have good relations in these communities, who then will alert law enforcement to a young man, mostly young men, who are susceptible to these blandishments.

And the use of the internet and the sophistication of these messages is very alarming. But I think, as time goes on, we are getting better and better about understanding the countermessage and how the countermessage differs by culture and by country.

Ms. KELLY. We don't talk much about the al-Nusra Front in Syria. What is our strategy to deal with that group of fighters?

Ambassador PATTERSON. The al-Nusra Front is an al-Qaeda affiliate. They are a designated terrorist organization. They have been successful on the battlefield in the north, and they have absorbed some, what I would call, non-extremist fighters because their own groups have been affected and because they, essentially, have nowhere else to go.

So, our strategy is that they are a terrorist group. They will not be part of any political settlement that is developed over time.

Ms. KELLY. I yield back the balance of my time. Thank you.

Mr. CONNOLLY. Would my friend yield?

Ms. KELLY. Yes.

Mr. CONNOLLY. I thank my friend.

Ambassador Nuland, I want to go back to the understandings with Russia. We had this meeting with 20 countries that the Secretary pulled together. Russia was there. Russia has been violating Turkish air space. Was there a discussion at that meeting and an understanding that Russia will cease and desist against our NATO ally?

Ambassador NULAND. The day of the Russian incursion into Turkish air space, the Secretary called Foreign Minister Lavrov immediately. As you know, the NATO Alliance also issued a strong statement of support for——

Mr. CONNOLLY. And did you get an assurance from the Russians they would cease and desist, was my question.

Ambassador NULAND. My understanding is that the Turks have now sought and gotten a reassurance from the Russians that they will cease and desist.

Mr. CONNOLLY. But not us in the Vienna meeting that we called together?

Ambassador NULAND. Well, we have made clear that it is unacceptable to be incurring NATO air space.

Mr. CONNOLLY. And did we do that in Vienna? Did we get any kind of assurance from the Russians?

Ambassador NULAND. Again, they have made clear to us that they do not intend to do it again, but, obviously, we have to watch they do rather than what they say.

Mr. CONNOLLY. Do we have any understanding in terms of rules of engagement with the Russians in terms of their military activities in Syria? This hearing is about Russia's escalation in Syria.

Ambassador NULAND. Congressman, in terms of direct negotiations, as you know, the Department of Defense conducted a very limited air de-confliction exercise with the Russians. We have an agreement on safe flight, which we have now tested, but we are not collaborating with them on where they can be and where we can be.

Mr. CONNOLLY. No, no. My question isn't collaboration. It is rules of engagement to make sure that there is not an inadvertent collision between our Air Force and theirs, our counselors and theirs, and the like.

Ambassador NULAND. That was the goal of this agreement, this Memorandum of Understanding, that we have now concluded, that we will stay away from each other. We have an emergency hotline. We have emergency communications——

Mr. CONNOLLY. So, they are in place? Okay.

Ambassador NULAND [continuing]. To protect our pilots, particularly because of the kind of flying that they do.

Mr. CONNOLLY. Thank you, and I thank my colleague for yielding.

Chairman ROYCE. Now we go to Mr. Randy Weber of Texas.

Mr. WEBER. Before I begin, Mr. Chairman, let me tell my friend Gerry Connolly I am not going to yield to you. You have gotten more time than all of us combined. Just kidding, Ger.

Ambassador Nuland, let me follow up with——

Mr. CONNOLLY. Were you yielding?

Mr. WEBER. No, no.

Ambassador Patterson, let me follow up with your exchange with Congressman Keating when he said that some of the generals have said the air war wouldn't do it at all, and you said you had been involved in those conversations. Do you recall that exchange earlier today?

Ambassador PATTERSON. Yes.

Mr. WEBER. Is the President aware of those conversations?

Ambassador PATTERSON. The President and our senior leadership meet very frequently on these issues, of course.

Mr. WEBER. How long have those conversations been going on?

Ambassador PATTERSON. Quite a while, Mr. Weber.

Mr. WEBER. A year? Two?

Ambassador PATTERSON. Easily. Easily.

Mr. WEBER. Okay. Just curious.

Ambassador Nuland, you said that Russia was spending $2.5 million per day on their military excursion into the Ukraine. I am sorry, we don't know what it is in the Ukraine, but into Syria. How long can they sustain that?

Ambassador NULAND. What I said was $2 million to $4 million a day, just to be clear.

Mr. WEBER. Okay.

Ambassador NULAND. And it may well be more than that. You know, in a country like Russia where there is only one prime decisionmaker, if Russia chooses to make this a priority over——

Mr. WEBER. Okay.

Ambassador NULAND [continuing]. The welfare of its own people, it could sustain it for some time.

Mr. WEBER. So, you have not calculated that? What is the U.S.'s outlay of expense on a day? Do we know that?

Ambassador PATTERSON. I'm dated, Mr. Weber, but the last time I asked, it was about $8 million a day.

Mr. WEBER. So, four times, or if you use the two, two to four times the amount Russia is using, but we are getting one-eighth the amount of airstrikes? Is that what I am to understand?

Ambassador PATTERSON. Mr. Weber, that would include Iraq, the entire air campaign. But, again, we are not the Russians.

Mr. WEBER. Okay.

Ambassador PATTERSON. And we have different standards.

Mr. WEBER. All right. And then, you said earlier—it might have been Ambassador Nuland—that the Gulf countries were not taking any refugees, but they had been very generous with their money. Was that you, Ambassador Patterson?

Ambassador PATTERSON. That's right.

Mr. WEBER. Okay.

Ambassador PATTERSON. That's right, Mr. Weber. I have the list of——

Mr. WEBER. Okay. Well, I am fascinated by my colleague Mo Brooks' idea of arming those in the Ukraine to maybe divert some of Russia's attention to increase, maybe to help defend Ukraine and to increase Russia's expense and cost, and maybe deflect them some from Syria.

If the Gulf countries are, as one of you said—I think you said it was you—are very generous with their money, would they help in that regard to arm some of the Ukrainians against the Russians? Has that question been raised to them?

Ambassador PATTERSON. As far as I know, that question has never risen, Mr. Weber.

Mr. WEBER. How about the question why won't they take refugees?

Ambassador PATTERSON. Because they have very different types of societies, and I know that——

Mr. WEBER. But they do want their society to continue as they know it, right? And if ISIL overruns their societies, it will be gone?

Ambassador PATTERSON. Yes, and they have a very—we have a very close degree of intelligence and military cooperation with our GCC, Gulf Cooperation partners, GCC partners. On cyber, on military, on intelligence, we have a very close relationship. So, yes, we work closely in anti-ISIL activity.

Mr. WEBER. But they could put up temporary camps if they are concerned about their society, tent cities, if you will, and they could actually take refugees and house them and feed them probably with a lot more money than some of the European nations, wouldn't you agree, if they were willing?

Ambassador PATTERSON. I am not sure that is true actually because the level of social services and infrastructure is vastly better in Europe. But, of course, we do want the Gulf to play a more active role and we do encourage them and we do want them to provide funding for these activities.

Mr. WEBER. Okay. Now what happens—and Gerry Connolly asked the question about what if there was a problem between the United States aircraft and the Russian aircraft—in your opinion, what is going to happen when the Russian aircraft drops, the Russian military drops a bomb on some of our 50 advisors over there? What happens?

Ambassador PATTERSON. Well, we have these de-confliction procedures in place, as Ambassador Nuland just outlined, these de-confliction procedures that they were designed to avoid any conflict between Russia and——

Mr. WEBER. If that happens, would our pilots be authorized to shoot that plane down that dropped the bomb?

Ambassador PATTERSON. I can't speculate on that.

Mr. WEBER. Ambassador Nuland, do you have any knowledge?

Ambassador NULAND. Without getting into classified information, I would simply say that where we anticipate these special operators being, the Russians have been very far from that territory because, as you know, these special operators are operating against, would be operating against ISIL. And our concern is that Russia is operating in support of Assad.

Mr. WEBER. Well, let's keep our fingers crossed.

I yield back.

Chairman ROYCE. Dr. Ami Bera of California.

Mr. BERA. Thank you, Mr. Chairman.

I am going to play off some of the comments that my colleague from Illinois, Ms. Kelly, talked about. Our goal is to defeat and destroy ISIL, and it is clear that we don't have the forces, but we have had some success in terms of the forces on the ground.

I think Ms. Kelly pointed out that the anti-ISIL coalitions killed about 10,000 ISIS fighters, and part of our challenge is that they are being replaced. We can have success, but some of it is stopping the replacement.

I think, Ambassador Patterson, you talked about doing what we can at the borders certainly, doing what we can on tracking the fighters that are leaving some of the North African countries, some of the Middle Eastern countries, and even some of the Western States.

I do think we are losing the propaganda war, though, right? I think ISIL has shown to be able to use the internet very efficiently, social media very efficiently. And maybe, Ambassador Patterson, this is a question for you. Are we doing enough to counter this propaganda war, to slow down their ability to recruit?

Ambassador PATTERSON. This is a big challenge, but I think we are getting better at it. For instance, we have a joint center with the United Arab Emirates and it has to be in Arabic and it has to be in an Arab country. They have begun to put out products that are designed to discourage mostly young men from joining ISIL.

We are working with a broad range, under General Allen's coalition, we have a working group on messaging. We have now a very large operation at the State Department and with the intelligence community that works on designing the most appropriate message for these individuals. So, I think we are making progress.

We are also making progress—let me take Tunisia. Tunisia has the most Jihadis per capita of any country in the world. But in the past year we have worked intensively with them on intelligence issues and countermessaging and training religious leaders to counter that message.

So, again, I certainly don't want to overstate this, but I think we have gotten better and are making at least some marginal progress.

Mr. BERA. I think I would echo—the chairman has certainly led us on a number of hearings here. We have to redouble our efforts on the propaganda war, because if we can stop it on the front end, we won't have to fight them on the battlefield. And I do think we are losing that front-end propaganda war through social media and the internet.

Ambassador Nuland, I would agree with you, very much so, that Russia's involvement is very counterproductive. It is exacerbating an already-challenging situation in Syria and certainly is escalating the refugee crisis and does threaten to wreak havoc in some of our allies, Jordan, Turkey. You are seeing our European allies struggle with this refugee crisis.

I know there has been some discussion—and it is not easy—about creating a safe zone within Syria and a no-fly zone within Syria where some of the Syrians that are fleeing some of the conflict zones can go. I would be curious about what it would take to potentially create that zone, Ambassador Patterson, or whoever.

Ambassador PATTERSON. It would take a massive commitment of air power. It would take a massive commitment of air power, and it would detract the air assets from the fight against ISIL. There is no option, Congressman, that has been put on the table so far within the administration that is considered viable because of the enormous resources that it would require to protect the population within it.

Mr. BERA. Okay. Great. Again, is that an option that is being discussed? Again, not an easy option, nothing about Syria is easy.

Ambassador PATTERSON. It is constantly being discussed and it is constantly under review, but that is the current status of it.

Mr. BERA. Okay. Great.

Mr. Chairman, I will yield back.

Chairman ROYCE. Thank you, Mr. Bera.

We now go to Ileana Ros-Lehtinen, our chairman emeritus.

Ms. ROS-LEHTINEN. Thank you so much, Mr. Chairman.

And welcome, Ambassadors.

I continue to be extremely frustrated by the administration's inability to implement or even articulate a strategy in Syria or in the Middle East as a whole. Despite the public facade, it does not appear that the President really wants Assad removed from power or that we have any understanding of the long-term tragic impact that Assad's policies are having on the Syrian people, on the region, our allies, on our national security, or else we know it and don't wish to do anything about it.

Do we really need additional evidence to prove that the current chaos is not working? The President seems to be running out the clock until it is someone else's problem, and I don't think history will look kindly on the choices that this administration has made on the Syria issue.

Some questions for you, and I would like to get yes-and-no answers, if I could. Do you believe that ISIL and Assad are separate issues?

Ambassador PATTERSON. No, at this point——

Ms. ROS-LEHTINEN. Thank you.

Ambassador PATTERSON [continuing]. Ms. Ros-Lehtinen, they are linked.

Ms. ROS-LEHTINEN. And do you agree that Assad's atrocities against his own people are a recruiting tool for ISIL?

Ambassador PATTERSON. Absolutely.

Ms. ROS-LEHTINEN. Is it possible to defeat ISIL while Assad's massacres continue with Iran and Russia's help?

Ambassador PATTERSON. No, the two issues are linked.

Ms. ROS-LEHTINEN. Is it possible to negotiate a solution with the opposition while they continue?

Ambassador PATTERSON. Possibly.

Ms. ROS-LEHTINEN. Are we pressuring Iran and Russia to stop Assad's massacre?

Ambassador PATTERSON. Absolutely, on a daily basis.

Ms. ROS-LEHTINEN. Should we infer that the President agrees more with Russia and Iran's goal of keeping Assad in power than he would have us believe?

Ambassador PATTERSON. Certainly not. The President and certainly the Secretary have said many times that Assad's departure is absolutely critical to any future in Syria.

Ms. ROS-LEHTINEN. What has the President and the White House, through the Secretary of State, communicated to you about the administration's desired end-state and national security objectives in Syria, and is it possible to achieve those goals when Russia and Iran's goals are the complete opposite?

Ambassador PATTERSON. The Secretary—of course, we have different goals in Syria—but I think the Secretary's goal is to find sufficient common ground through a process of negotiation and a political settlement, that we might be able to find a way through this. He is not naive about this. This is what the whole Vienna process and followup process is about.

Ms. ROS-LEHTINEN. And when you say common ground and a political settlement, does that entail keeping Assad in power?

Ambassador PATTERSON. No, absolutely not, but it might entail some negotiation on a timetable for his departure.

Ms. ROS-LEHTINEN. And we would be working with who to try to achieve that settlement to have him go somewhere else?

Ambassador PATTERSON. We are working with—in the Vienna process are 20 different countries. Obviously, our Gulf allies and the Turks. The Turks are intimately involved with this, as are some of our European allies. And we are constantly in touch with the U.N. and members of the moderate opposition and armed opposition within Syria and those civilian leaders in exile.

Ms. ROS-LEHTINEN. Those allies, do they see Assad's removal from power as imperative to deal with this situation?

Ambassador PATTERSON. Certainly our European allies, our Gulf allies, and Turkey do see that. They are absolutely determined that he will not remain in power.

Ms. ROS-LEHTINEN. And to follow up on Ms. Frankel's questions, there is a lot of talk in different communities that we represent about whether the United States is doing enough to protect Syrian civilians from the Assad regime. Is that still one of the priorities of this administration, and how is that priority manifested?

Ambassador PATTERSON. Certainly we try. We have provided over $2 billion, $2.5 billion, for humanitarian assistance inside Syria. So, we are certainly trying to feed and support Syrian populations who are under great stress.

And we have certainly, as you mentioned, raised before, we have certainly talked with the Russians about preventing Assad from attacking his own people.

Ms. ROS-LEHTINEN. And the bombs that we have seen that have been attacking some of the forces with whom we are dealing and we are protecting and we are arming, and yet, some of those airstrikes seem to be targeting the very folks who are supposed to be the good guys in this battle. What are we doing to make sure that that ends?

Ambassador PATTERSON. That is absolutely true, Congresswoman. We mentioned, I think, that 85 to 90 percent of the strikes were against anti-regime forces.

And on your second question, we can talk more about that in a classified setting.

Ms. ROS-LEHTINEN. Just one last question; I know I am out of time. There has been a lot of discussion in the open press about like-minded factors like the al-Nusra Front being part of this coalition that will, then, defeat another band of bad guys. Are we in that coalition-building with folks who we would normally see as our enemies and the enemies of our values?

Ambassador PATTERSON. Nusra Front is an al-Qaeda affiliate. It is possible that some members of the opposition have been forced to adhere, to join to al-Nusra because they had nowhere else to go. The al-Nusra Front and its leadership are terrorist groups.

Ms. ROS-LEHTINEN. And we will remain with that thinking and not help those groups with their alliances with other——

Ambassador PATTERSON. No, we have designated Nusra.

Ms. ROS-LEHTINEN. Thank you. Thank you very much.

Thank you, Mr. Chairman.

Chairman ROYCE. Thank you, Ileana.

We go now to David Cicilline of Rhode Island.

Mr. CICILLINE. Thank you to our witnesses for being here and, of course, for your service.

But I have to tell you I remain very concerned that the absence of a coherent strategy for success in Syria and Iraq to defeat ISIL, and further complicated by Russian escalation and really a failure to define what success is, continues to really plague us in Syria. Of course, the best way to press the administration and Congress to do this is to vigorously debate an authorization for the use of military force, during which the President would be required to articulate a strategy and to persuade both the American people and Congress of the likelihood of success of that strategy.

And I recognize this is complicated. There are not easy answers. But I think it is compounded. Frankly, Ambassador Patterson, in your written testimony you indicate that our strategy in the Syrian conflict remains the same, essentially using diplomacy and military action to achieve a political transition. Of course, that is not a strategy; that is a goal.

And so, I think what we are really looking for and what we need is a detailed plan of action with goals and a plan to mobilize resources to achieve those goals. That is really a strategy. I think that is really what we are missing and what I think is critical.

But I want to ask some very specific questions. You said, Ambassador Patterson, in your testimony that the coalition has made progress in our military campaign against ISIL. But, according to Al Arabiya, as of October of this year, ISIL controls half of all the territory in Syria as opposed to July 2014, when they controlled about a third of Syrian territory.

So, first, is that correct, that ISIL, in fact, controls more territory now than they did in the summer of 2014? And if so, how is that progress?

Ambassador PATTERSON. I think they do, they may control more land territory, but certainly there has been progress against ISIL in Tikrit and Bayji, in the efforts in Ramadi. Again, there has been considerable progress against the leadership. The top of my head, I think 60 leaders of ISIL, including some very important ones, have been taken off the battlefield. The effort by Special Forces against Abu Sayyaf, who was a leader of ISIL, and against his wife was an intelligence bonanza. So, there has been progress, but, as the President and everybody else has said, this is obviously going to be a multi-year campaign that is going to require consider resources to prosecute.

Mr. CICILLINE. With respect to the moderate opposition, there has been a lot of discussion about supporting the moderate opposition and that appears to be at least a tactic in our Syrian response. Who is the moderate opposition? The President has just authorized another $100 million expenditure, so now totaling $500 million. There are reports that there are as many as 1,000 armed militia groups and that much of the success of the larger groups, the FSA, comes about as a result of working alongside some of the most hard-line groups. So, who are we talking about when we are speaking about moderate opposition and do they, in fact, include elements of al-Qaeda and al-Nusra and other more extremist groups?

Ambassador PATTERSON. Well, let me take the civilian moderate opposition, too, and that is the assistance figure that you are referring to. That is groups within Syria and groups that live in Turkey and Lebanon and other places.

What that project is designed to do is to keep these people not only alive physically, but also keep them viable for a future Syria. Because we have managed to, even areas under control of ISIL— I won't mention them—but we have managed to provide money to city councils, to health clinics, to teachers and policemen. So, these people can still provide public services and form the basis for a new Syria. That is a good portion of that money goes into efforts like that.

There is also the opposition on the ground. I think they have sort of gotten a bum rap in this hearing because I think they are more extensive than is generally recognized, particularly in the south. And, yes, of course, in the north, some of these individuals have affiliated with Nusra because there was nowhere else to go. But I think there is a wide range of moderate commanders that we have worked with closely, and I think they are viable and will be able to play a part in the future of Syria.

Mr. CICILLINE. Finally, the President, obviously, has just announced 50 Special Forces will be dispatched to Syria to advise and assist Kurdish forces in that region. Can you tell me what the end-goal of this is? What is the objective? How can we be sure that this limited deployment doesn't begin a very slippery slope and a wider, deeper military engagement in the Syrian civil war?

Finally, you mentioned the financial support of the Gulf nations for the refugees. We have heard from a number of refugee organizations that there is not sufficient financial support from Gulf countries. I know you mentioned Qatar, but are there other countries in the Gulf that are not doing as much as they should? Because we are hearing a very different representation from refugee organizations that are charged with actually dealing with the crisis on the ground.

Ambassador PATTERSON. Let me provide you right after this hearing with a list of support I have from the Gulf. I think some of the traditional refugee agencies, there is not enough money. There is simply not enough money for this enormous humanitarian catastrophe. Let me stress that.

But I think the Gulf nations have both been generous with the U.N. and often their money is put through local Red Cross and Red Crescent societies, their local NGOs and PVOs. And so, perhaps there is some concern about that, that they are not going through the big international NGOs. But I will provide you with that.

Mr. CICILLINE. And what about the 50——

Ambassador PATTERSON. On the 50, we talked a lot about the strategy of ground support and working with partners. These 50 Special Forces are to work with the Syrian Arab Coalition, which has had considerable success in closing the border, and to improve their capacity. I think, anything else, we will provide it to you in a classified letter.

Mr. CICILLINE. Thank you, and I yield back, Mr. Chairman.

Chairman ROYCE. Thank you, Mr. Cicilline.

We go now to Mr. Dana Rohrabacher of California.

Mr. ROHRABACHER. Thank you very much.

Let me just say that I am very frustrated by talk about Russia. I spent my entire life trying to defeat the Soviet Union, and I was very pleased to be part of the Reagan administration that helped accomplish that goal of bringing down a regime that wanted to impose an atheist dictatorship throughout the world in order to promote their ideology.

And Russians expect to be treated as friends, the Russian people, after the fall of communism. And what has risen instead is a hostility that is just so overwhelming that it is damaging, not only has been damaging Russia and their ability to establish themselves in a new world role, because it is, after all, a major power in the world and they have interests. No matter if they are not communists at all, they are a major power with interests, just as we are.

But the double standard that we have been judging Russia, and even is present in the hearing today, is just overwhelming. We sit here and say, ''Oh, well, Russia wants to keep Assad in power, how horrible that is because Assad is a dictatorship,'' as if Saudi Arabia isn't a dictatorship and wouldn't murder millions of people or thousands of people to stay in power. What about the other Gulf states run by kingdoms who would murder their people in great number? They are no different than Assad. In fact, they might be better than Assad because some of them are religiously-motivated to the point that it was sort of like communism was a religious conviction; well, their form of Islam sometimes puts them at odds with Sunnis or Shiites killing each other.

The double standard that we have been judging Russia with, and basing our policy on that double standard, has caused us great harm. Great harm. Putin 5 years ago tried to work out a compromise with us, and we turned him down, that would have created at least some sort of semblance of stability in Syria. And now, it has totally gone to hell, and we still can't get ourselves to try to look at Putin as a possible partner in cooperation to make things better.

I believe it is our hostility toward Russia that has prevented us from creating a policy that will create a more stable Middle East. And Gaddafi, we made an agreement with him about Gaddafi. And what did we do? We broke that agreement, and has that resulted in order to have the alternative, the non-Gaddafi, non-Islamic alternatives into power, did that make it any better there? No. Libya today, half of Libya is controlled by people who want to murder us because they are radical Muslims.

Had we been working with the Russians all along in good faith, I believe this situation in the Middle East would have been totally different and better, stayed more stable. And let me just note that I can remember the charges, the monstrous charges against us in Iraq, how horrible it was; our troops were murdering people by the thousands. Most of those reports were false, were wrong. They were lies by people who wanted to achieve a political end by claiming that we were massacring people intentionally in Iraq.

Well, I don't know, is it possible that some of these reports that we are getting—yes, Assad is a murderous dictator, but some of the magnitude of his oppression and his murder of his own people might be exaggerated to achieve certain political ends. I would think so.

We have a little time to answer. Let me give you a question, so you can—please feel free to disagree with everything that I say. I believe it, and I know you have your beliefs, too, and they are honest disagreements.

But let me just ask, then, about, if, indeed, Assad is removed and we get this third alternative, why won't it be just the same as happened with Gaddafi, where the radical Islamists who hate us now see a weaker adversary, and it will come in and replace whatever that regime is very quickly with a regime that will control all of Syria and they will be radicals that will be our worst nightmare? Why wouldn't that happen in Syria the way it happened in Libya?

Ambassador PATTERSON. I need to say something, Mr. Rohrabacher.

Mr. ROHRABACHER. Please feel free to retort what I said.

Ambassador PATTERSON. With respect, I can't let it go by, the comparison of Bashar al-Assad with our Gulf allies. These countries are not in our image, but there is no way that they oppress their citizens or kill their citizens to the extent that Bashar al-Assad is.

But let me——

Mr. ROHRABACHER. You are saying they wouldn't do that? They would not engage in use of the military to suppress their people if their guest workers decided to rise up?

Ambassador PATTERSON. Yes, I am saying that, Mr. Rohrabacher.

Mr. ROHRABACHER. They wouldn't? That is very naive.

Ambassador PATTERSON. Saudi Arabia is a country I know well, and they would not do that. That is not how it works there.

But let me try to answer your question about Syria. There is broad consensus in the international community that the institutions in Syria would remain intact, the intelligence, the military, the police, the civil service, the ministerial structures, and that the goal is to remove Bashar al-Assad and his closest advisors and have ths political process that would lead to a new government. So, it is not to destroy the institutional structure.

In Libya, I would argue there weren't any institutions.

Mr. ROHRABACHER. Okay. You have outlined it well.

Ambassador PATTERSON. It is a very different——

Mr. ROHRABACHER. You have outlined it well.

Why do we have to go in and make that decision in Syria? Why is it for the United States to step into this far-off land rather than going to perfect—there are lots of places we could go and perfect. Why is it for us to have to go in and do that when we know that you have got these radical Islamists who are just waiting on the sideline for some type of instability that they could take advantage of?

Ambassador PATTERSON. Because our national security is at stake in the region, and the security of our allies like Israel and the GCC countries and Lebanon and Jordan, Turkey, is ultimately affected by what happens in Syria.

Mr. ROHRABACHER. That's right, and our policies are making the instability worse. In fact, dealing with Putin instead of trying to demonize him, perhaps we could have had more stability there and our friends would be actually better off than the current policy of, whatever we do, don't work with Russia and get rid of Assad. Putin is also helping us, by the way, with the General el-Sisi who we only give just lip service to try to help the man who has a pivotal role in stability in the Middle East.

Chairman ROYCE. We need to go to Grace Meng of New York. The time has expired.

Ms. MENG. Thank you, Mr. Chairman, and thank you to our witnesses for being here and all that you do for our country.

My question is about growing concern of advanced Russian arms entering Syria at unprecedented levels and the possibility for advanced arms to pass to Syrian forces and even to groups like Hezbollah, which is high. What is the U.S. prepared to do to counter this? What have we done? What could we do more of to ensure these Russian arms don't end up in the hands of Hezbollah?

Ambassador NULAND. Well, we have the same concerns that you do about the advanced weaponry flowing into Syria from Russia, from Iran. We have raised these concerns regularly with the Russians, including at the Presidential level, and we are continuing to monitor what exactly happens with them. The Russians, as you know, have now made a decision to put in ground artillery, and that is exacerbating the conflict further in Hama and in Homs.

Ms. MENG. My second question is, Russia has conducted a number of airstrikes on rebel locations in the Syrian Golan, some strikes which are only about 30 to 40 miles from the Israeli border. Iran has also sent troop and military advisors to shore up Assad's rule, including on the Golan Heights, bringing Iran's influence directly to Israel's doorstep. Jihadist groups, including ISIS and al-Nusra, also continue to gain territory in northern and souther Syrian, including along the Golan Heights.

In your opinion, how likely is it that fighting in Syria could spill over into Israel and what are the major concerns from the Israelis? And what can the U.S. do to help?

Ambassador PATTERSON. Congresswoman, nothing is more important to us as a national strategic interest than Israel's security. And all these elements that you have raised, the Russian strikes, the pressure on Nusra in the Golan Heights, the Iranian presence, we are in constant contact with the Israeli Government and are working very collaboratively on this.

I would say the Israelis can pretty much take care of this problem, and they have shown that in a number of ways that we can perhaps discuss later. But we have lots of collaboration on this issue.

And on a broader issue, the Prime Minister, of course, will be here. We have given millions of dollars, billions of dollars, including Iron Dome, over the past 3 years. We will be discussing ways that we can enhance Israel's security generally, but these are concerns that we share with Israel and we meet with them and address them in all kinds of ways.

Ms. MENG. Thank you. I yield back.

Mr. McCAUL [presiding]. Thank you.

My question, first on Syria and, then, Iran. I have been briefed on the target packages in Syria. I think as you indicated, let me say, first of all, when you don't have a strategy and you fail to have a strategy, you end up with a power vacuum. And now, we have Russia filling that power vacuum, not unlike the terrorists do. And now, it has really created a complicated situation, from my perspective.

When I look at the target packages of Russian strikes, as you mentioned, 90 percent are anti-Assad; only 10 percent are even remotely targeted toward ISIS. It raises a question of, why is Russia there? What is their intent?

I have talked to our partners in the Middle East. Some say that Russia has told them it is to defeat ISIS, and then, others tell me that the only reason they are there is to support the Assad regime.

Very briefly, what do you believe is Russia's intent in the region?

Ambassador PATTERSON. Well, I think their main intent—they have several intents—but their main intent was to shore up Bashar al-Assad. He was losing ground, significant ground, when they decided to come in. They also want to protect their interests in Tartus. They want to reassert themselves, as Ambassador Nuland said. But their primary interest was to shore up Bashar al-Assad.

Mr. McCAUL. I tend to agree with that, and here is the problem that this now presents: You know, 50 Special Forces guys, they are our best, but that is not going to win the day. And I would argue they are in harm's way right now.

If there was a strategy, it was the Sunni fighting the Sunni extremists. When I talk to nations like Turkey and Jordan and the Gulf states, they are willing to put a ground force in there to defeat ISIS, but they would never do so if it emboldened and empowered Assad. And that was kind of part of the agreement.

Now that the Russians are in there backing Assad, it doesn't look like he is going anywhere anytime soon. So, where do we get our ground force now?

Ambassador PATTERSON. Ambassador Nuland can speak more about this. We have been working very closely on an enhanced effort with the Turks to close the border. As I mentioned, the Syrian Air Coalition, which will be supported by our Special Forces, and, frankly, Mr. McCaul, we have had lots of discussions with our Gulf allies and with Jordan about the possibility of introducing ground troops. I think they have probably told you that, too. So, that is the status of that at this point. We work very closely with the Jordanians about the issues in southern Syria.

Mr. McCAUL. Jordan has been one of our best friends in the region. But, again, it is going to be difficult to get a Sunni ground force now that Assad is not part of the—it is going to be difficult to get Assad out now that the Russians are in there.

Ambassador PATTERSON. Let me stress that that is our goal, to get Assad out. We don't think the Russians are going to have such an easy walk through Syria with the opposition of the entire Sunni world. So, there may be a political opening here that we can exploit to move him out.

Mr. McCAUL. I think if you could reach a political reconciliation, and perhaps even partition the Alawite from the rest of the country, that is a possibility. Right now, it is about de-confliction with the Russians, so we don't kill each other over there.

Do you foresee any remote possibility of a joint strategy to defeat ISIS with the Russians?

Ambassador NULAND. The only way we would end up in a joint strategy is if the Russians agreed to the general premise that we have to have a ceasefire, we have to have a transitional government, and we have to have a decision on getting rid of Assad. That is what the Secretary has been working on. In the meantime, we are working on ISIS and they are working in a different part of this area to defend Assad. So, I don't see working together militarily unless and until it is all efforts on a transition, and that would allow us, in turn, to focus good Syrian forces on——

Mr. McCAUL. Of course. And I would be very careful in trusting them. But I will tell you, based on the Boston bombing experience, I learned that we have a common enemy, and that is the Jihadists. The Chechen rebels, we know there are thousands of them joining ISIS. I predict that Russia is going to have a homeland security problem of their own, and as that becomes more of a problem for them, their desire to move away from protecting the regime to attacking ISIS, hopefully, will shift.

Ambassador NULAND. I think that is what is so frustrating to us, is that we ought to share a goal of defeating ISIS and defeating those who come from Russia to join ISIS, but that is not what the Russian military is currently focused on.

Mr. McCAUL. My last question is with respect to Iran. We have reached this agreement, which I disagreed with, but, nevertheless, it is moving forward. Since that time, Iran has taken several provocative actions, including ballistic missile tests, the jailing of Americans on frivolous charges, and support for terrorist activities via the IRGC, the Iranian Revolutionary Guard Corps.

The Quds Force is the terrorist arm of Iran. I sent a letter to the President of the United States requesting that the IRGC be placed on the foreign terrorist organization list because they are the terror arm of Iran. This would not lift the sanctions. It would keep the sanctions in place on the very terrorist activities that Iran wants to take the $100 billion and shift them toward these activities.

What is your response to whether or not designating the IRGC as an FTO, whether that is a good decision?

Ambassador PATTERSON. I am virtually certain they are already subject to sanctions, aren't they, Mr. McCaul? Yes, the IRGC——

Mr. McCAUL. Well, they are not designated as a foreign terrorist organization, which would make a difference.

Ambassador PATTERSON. I can't answer that question, Mr. McCaul. I will have to get back to you. I would not think they would meet the legal criteria, but I don't really know. We will get back to you.

Mr. McCAUL. I would think that IRGC, with the Quds Force being the main sponsor of terror within Iran, would qualify to be a foreign terrorist organization, though.

Ambassador Nuland?

Ambassador NULAND. Again, I defer to Anne on the questions involving Iran.

Mr. McCAUL. Well, I look forward to the President's response. To date, I have not received one at this time.

The Chair now recognizes Mr. Sherman.

Mr. SHERMAN. It is always good to have you here. We hear folks say, ''Where's your strategy?'' That implies that the United States is in control of events, that we own them, that the outcome is determined by what goes on here in Washington. That is a very dangerous viewpoint.

We can be a force for good, but to control the outcome, I would ask anybody to put forward a strategy that would lead us to peace, stability, and democracy in Iraq and Syria with modest American casualties and modest American cost. George W. Bush had a strategy to achieve that for Iraq. It failed.

In the future, those who say, ''Where's your strategy?'' are really saying, ''Why can't you control the world at no cost?'' And that is a silly question.

We are told by the gentlelady from Florida that the evils of Assad deliver recruits to ISIS. That is correct. But we should point out that the actions of Maliki and many who are still in the Baghdad regime do just as much to help ISIS recruit. Just because the government in Baghdad was installed by us doesn't mean it is part of the solution; it is part of the problem. And we ought to be looking very carefully at our aid to Baghdad when The Wall Street Journal can put on the front page how so many 100 dollar bills, amounting to tens of billions of dollars, are shipped from Washington and disappearing in Iraq, except they are turning up with ISIS.

Ambassador Patterson, I have one little bit of advice for you, but, also, it will help the other bureaus next to you. And that is you ought to hire a couple of folks who are experts in Islamic theology, the Hadith, Islamic jurisprudence. You cannot understand and you cannot argue and you cannot persuade if you do not understand the mindset of both our friends and enemies, both of whom are drawing.

If you need Congress to say not everybody has to pass the Foreign Service Exam—one or two experts—because the Foreign Service Exam does not ask the difference between a good Hadith and a bad Hadith. I know. So, you need some experts in this, both to talk to our friends and understand our enemies.

As to chemical weapons, the administration achieved a major victory in getting all chemical weapons out, or virtually all out of Syria. Now chlorine remains. Hell, chlorine is next to every pool in my district. You can't prohibit chlorine. It is unfortunate that chlorine has been used illegally as a weapon. But those chemicals that are illegal per se appear to have been removed from Syria. I won't say you had a great plan or a great strategy, but you did have a great result on that issue.

The solution to the refugee crisis is peace in Syria, not to cancel Syria and move its population to Europe. We had a policy that many of us pushed here in Congress to arm the reasonable elements in Syria. That policy has basically failed. It has failed for a couple of reasons. First, you did it years after we started pushing for it. But, second, it is still subject to the incredible and ridiculous condition that those we arm have to convince us that they do not intend to fight Assad. Any reasonable patriotic Syrian intends to fight Assad. So, no wonder we only find 50 people and we only have five on the battlefield. How do you find somebody who is reasonable who doesn't hate Assad?

And I will point out that, while ISIS has the bad taste to put its murders right there on television, beheadings, it is the Shiite Alliance of Iran and Assad that pose the greater threat to the United States. They have killed far more innocent people and have killed far more Americans.

Now, turning to Russia, Russia is not in a terribly strong position, $45-a-barrel oil. They cannot waste resources on peripheral matters. The Ukraine is of vital national interest to Russia. If it fails to protect Russian-speaking persons, Putin is gone. And if the Ukraine is successful, it becomes a model inspiring all Russians to change and follow that model, given the very close history between the Ukraine and Russia.

Syrian, contrast, is not at the center of Russia's universe. There are substantial costs to what Russia is doing. Syria and Assad are very close to the center of Iran's national security. They dream of a Shiite control from Mashhad in eastern Iran to Latakia on the Mediterranean.

Assad has been their longest ally. So, one would raise the question, not why is Iran doing what they are doing, but why is Russia? And then, we look at the timing. Russia deployed forces, at substantial long-term risk and cost to Russia, a couple of days after it became certain to those who are observing things, especially here in Congress, that Iran would get its hands on the $130 billion. First, they had to sign the agreement. Until that, they might not get their money.

Then, you had to look around here and make sure Congress wasn't going to blow up the agreement. Well, it was pretty apparent that we were not going to blow up the agreement a few weeks after it was signed. And it was pretty much like a day or two after a lot of us concluded that Congress was not going to prevent this agreement from going into effect for the first couple of years, that Iran was going to get its hands on the money, that Russia started effort.

So, the question is, if Iran is giving the money to Assad, so he can give money to Russia, or if Iran is sending the money directly to Russia, would we know about it? So, I will ask both of you, since one focuses on Iran and the Middle East and one on Europe, if there was a transfer of $1 billion from Tehran to Moscow, either through Damascus or otherwise, would we know about it and would it be public?

Ambassador NULAND. Congressman, I don't think at this stage we have seen any evidence of payments to Russia. On the contrary, we see Russia hemorrhaging money on its latest adventure in Syria.

Mr. SHERMAN. But if there was a transfer—and, obviously, Iran doesn't quite have its hands on the money yet; so Putin is going to have to wait a little while—but if there was a transfer of $1 billion this winter, are you confident that you would know about it?

Ambassador PATTERSON. Let me answer that as not confident, but I think the chances are pretty good.

Mr. SHERMAN. Pretty good you would know? Well, okay.

And, Ambassador Nuland?

Ambassador NULAND. Well, if it was in any dollar-denominated form, we would likely know. But if they wanted to do a bushel of Iranian currency or rubles, maybe not.

Mr. SHERMAN. Or euros.

Ambassador NULAND. Euros I think we would know, yes.

Mr. SHERMAN. You would know about a transfer of $1 billion? So, let me, then, ask: Obviously, North Korea was paid $1 billion, $½ billion, for Al Kibar and the tremendous aid that they provided to a Syrian or a Syrian/Iranian nuclear program. Did we know about that? Or did the Israelis bring to us the fact that Al Kibar was a nuclear site many years after North Korea received payment?

Ambassador PATTERSON. I don't know the answer to that, Mr. Sherman. I know that we have extremely close cooperation with the Israelis. They have sources that we don't have. I just don't know the answer.

Mr. SHERMAN. Well, Israel spotted the location; nobody spotted the money. And so, the confidence that bad guys can't move money without us knowing or that Russia is financing this without being paid by Iran is untested.

I yield back.

Mr. PERRY [presiding]. The Chair thanks the gentleman.

The Chair recognizes itself for questions.

Thank you, Ambassadors, for being here.

The use of DoD of these 50 Special Operators, lo, the other folks that aren't characterized as boots on the ground, is an extension of diplomacy through means of exacting the policy that we would like to see happen in the Middle East or anywhere. It is just an extension. I think if you would kind of see it in those terms, it is cross listed.

With that in mind, because it keeps on being stated that this is not a combat mission, so is there anywhere in the mix that State Department is in the chain of command and decisionmaking at all for what these Special Operators or people that wear a military uniform or are paid by the Department of Defense acting in Syria and Iraq in this operation, is there any State Department involvement in the decisionmaking process about what they do, where they go, and how they conduct their business?

Ambassador PATTERSON. Yes, absolutely, Mr. Chairman. First of all, the State Department, through the Secretary, through General Allen who was coming to the State Department, participate in all these discussions and they work closely with the Turkish Government to work on the effort to close the border. And these Special Forces Advisors are critical to that effort. So, yes, we have been deeply involved in that.

Mr. PERRY. You are involved in the chain of command? So, do you do——

Ambassador PATTERSON. Currently not, sir. They are not the chain of command, but the overall policy process, and particularly there have been State Department representatives, General Allen, now Brett McGurk, and others, on these teams, Ambassador Nuland, who have discussed these efforts at great length with the Turks.

Mr. PERRY. To come to some conclusion, and then, the military command makes the decisions and issues the orders commensurate with what you have come up with?

Ambassador PATTERSON. Commensurate with what the President of the United States comes up with and instructs them to do. But, of course, these Special Forces Advisors are under the command of General Lloyd Austin.

Mr. PERRY. Okay. So, what is their mission? These 50, up to 50, is what I hear, up to 50 Special Ops, what is their mission?

Ambassador NULAND. Congressman, with respect, I think that is a question that we are going to defer to DoD and defer in a classified session probably.

Mr. PERRY. I mean, you have had the discussions, right? You just said you had the discussions, but you can't tell me the mission right now and that is classified. Yet, in everything I read, it is to advise and assist. I expected you to say, ''advise and assist.'' Is that not their mission?

Ambassador PATTERSON. Yes, it is to advise and assist, but what we can't sit here and tell you, Mr. Chairman, is where these fellows are going to be deployed, exactly whom they are going to be working with, exactly how many are going to be on the ground.

Mr. PERRY. Okay. I didn't ask you any of that, but I appreciate it. All right.

Ambassador PATTERSON. But advise and assist.

Mr. PERRY. So, advise and assist to what end? What is the goal?

Ambassador PATTERSON. The goal is to enhance our efforts to defeat ISIL, and we would be happy to give you a broader briefing on this.

Mr. PERRY. I mean, I think I understand it, but I want to make sure——

Ambassador PATTERSON. To close the border. To close the border, sir. To close the border, so ISIL can't get recruits and ISIL can't export refined products, and to put pressure on Raqqah, which is basically ISIL headquarters.

Mr. PERRY. This goes to a larger strategy. So, if you are telling me it is to achieve, the goal is to close the border and somehow at some point defeat ISIS—I don't want to put words in your mouth, but that is what I see; that is what I hear. Close the border. Defeat ISIS.

All right. We have got 50 guys that are going. Does that just strengthen Assad? Right? So, he has got ISIS and he has got local Sunni insurgents that are fighting him. And we take ISIS—let's just say in a perfect world everything in the strategy that we have, if you want to call it that, that we with these 50 guys defeat ISIS. Doesn't that strengthen Assad?

Ambassador PATTERSON. You can't solve the problem of ISIL separate from the problem of Assad.

Mr. PERRY. I understand that, but——

Ambassador PATTERSON. Okay.

Mr. PERRY. Okay. But tell me what happens if—let's just say the perfect thing happens, that you get what you want and our 50 operators, in conjunction with the Kurds and whoever they are working with, assisting and advising, defeat ISIS. Is Assad strengthened or he is weakened? He has Russia there right behind him right now attacking the very people that we have trained and are supporting.

Ambassador PATTERSON. You have to do both.

Mr. PERRY. But we are not doing both. We are doing one. Right?

Ambassador PATTERSON. We fighting ISIL and we are trying to get a political settlement to get President Assad——

Mr. PERRY. Okay. So, you don't want to answer that. But I would say that it does empower and increase the power of Assad. It does that.

And so, with all due respect to the gentleman that was just sitting here when he says there is no strategy, and you people that say that there is no strategy, and that the strategy assumes that we can control everything from the United States, that is absurd. We had a strategy in World War II. We couldn't control the Emperor of Japan or the Fuhrer or Stalin, but we had a strategy, and sometimes we had to deviate and adapt, but we had a strategy. I would say this is not a strategy, but that is my contention.

Now I am going to take some liberties here because everybody else seems to have done that. The President has said, his White House Press Secretary said that this is not a combat mission, right? Is Syria a combat zone? I mean, they are dropping bombs and they are shooting each other. Is it a combat zone or isn't it?

Ambassador PATTERSON. An extremely complex battlefield, and what the President said is what you just quoted back to me, Mr. Chairman, that it was an advise-and-assist movement.

Mr. PERRY. Right. So, they are not to patrol or travel with opposition groups. But it also says that it could change as the situation dictates. Now I expect to tell me, because I am going to ask you, what would change, what changes would dictate, what situation would dictate them changing that not patrolling or traveling with? But you are going to tell me that that is a classified setting.

Ambassador PATTERSON. Oh, I am not going to tell you that. I am going to tell you that I don't know and that is up to the President of the United States and the situation. Of course, he always reserves the right to change the role of American forces.

Mr. PERRY. Let me ask you this: If this isn't a combat zone and these forces are not on a combat mission, how is it that in May Delta Force Commandos entered Syria aboard helicopters and Ospreys and killed an Islamic State leader and about a dozen militant fighters, and one of our soldiers was killed just about a week and a half ago? If that is not a combat, what is that?

Ambassador PATTERSON. That is, that was a—Sergeant Wheeler grew up 20 miles from where I am from—that was a mission to save Kurdish hostages and other hostages. They rescued——

Ambassador PATTERSON. I know that, but you understand, when we imperil—these young men and women raised their hand and said they are going to defend the Constitution against all enemies, foreign and domestic, and pledge their lives, and it is with the proviso that the Commander-in-Chief and that the administration and the powers who be are going to sacrifice their lives for nothing. And these people are going into combat. We are saying it is not combat, but, indeed, it is combat.

Ambassador PATTERSON. Mr. Chairman, of course it is combat. These people go into combat because the President of the United States orders them into combat.

Mr. PERRY. That's right, they go into combat. Somebody loses their life and they don't come home with a Purple Heart because they weren't in combat. They don't come back with the correct SGLI because they weren't in combat. Do you understand the ramifications of pledging your life and pledging their lives? It is important.

Just a couple of other things. Because I reject the whole situation of the gentleman next to me who said there was no strategy, that those of us that said there was no strategy didn't have a strategy, that is absurd. There isn't a strategy. This is all tactics. And that George W. Bush didn't have a strategy, you might not have agreed with it, and I might not have agreed with it at times, but there was a strategy.

And I would also reject that the war in Iraq destabilized the area. Up until the President left Iraq, it was pretty stable. It was pretty stable. It wasn't perfect, but it wasn't what it is now.

With that, I will recognize Mr. Trott. Thank you.

Mr. TROTT. I want to thank the chair and, also, thank both of you for being here today and for everything you do for our country.

Ambassador Patterson, would you say our policy in the last 4 years has been a success in Syria?

Ambassador PATTERSON. I would say we have not succeeded in removing Bashar al-Assad from power, and I would say that ISIL is not defeated, but it will be a long, hard struggle to defeat ISIL.

Mr. TROTT. And do you think that insouciance on the part of the administration has contributed to our failure or not really impacted it? I mean, has the inability to make a decision a few years back complicated where we are today?

Ambassador PATTERSON. I don't want to speculate on that, Mr. Trott. I don't know and I wasn't around when those decisions were made, and I don't want to speculate. We are where we are now.

Mr. TROTT. Right. So, let's look forward. The policy going forward is we are going to have 50 Special Forces. We are going to continue with the airstrikes, and we have heard a lot of criticism of our policy there. Last week, you know, one day Russia attacked 94 targets; we attacked one.

We are going to start and have been calling out Russia for violating international law with respect to the rules of engagement.

We are going to ask Assad to stop dropping barrel bombs on his citizens. We are going to have meetings about a transitional government. Iran will be at the table. Opposition groups may or may not be.

And this strategy, as best I can discern this morning, is going to work because this is too complex for Russia. They are going to lose interest. They are going to run out of money, and it is just too difficult. Is that a fair statement of our strategy going forward? And if it isn't, please enlighten me as to how you believe the strategy is different than what I just described.

Ambassador PATTERSON. I think our strategy is—no, I don't think that is a fair characterization of our strategy.

Mr. TROTT. I mean, I have heard a number of times today Russia really isn't going to be in it for the long haul. They don't have the money. They have other problems. This is not a strategic interest that they want to put resources behind.

So, it seems to me that the gamble we are taking going forward is our strategy is going to succeed because Russia is going to lose interest. Tell me what I missed.

Ambassador PATTERSON. Well, no, our strategy is to mobilize the rest of the international community, including our Gulf allies and Turkey, to work toward a political solution and to work hard to defeat ISIL. I think the contributions on the defeat of ISIL and the efforts we are taking, which aren't just the 50 Special Forces, but also the strengthening of our position at Incirlik and the steps we are taking in Iraq will all accelerate the defeat the ISIL. So, that is a key element of this that has sort of been, in my view, underplayed in this hearing.

Mr. TROTT. Ambassador Patterson, you said earlier we are talking to the Russians. So, I have two questions. Are they listening? I know we have the MOU that was entered into last month. So, that is perhaps evidence that they are listening. But are they really listening to what our objectives and goals are? And what evidence do you have that the fact that we are taking to the Russians is moving them around on what our different goals are in Syria?

Ambassador NULAND. Congressman, as we have said throughout the morning, the conversations we have been having with them have not affected their military choices. They have not changed their pattern of bombing. They have also not taken us up on our insistence that a minimum price for their support for Assad ought to be to get him to stop barrel-bombing.

So, on the military side, I would say that they are not listening. They also are not listening to the Gulf Arabs. They are not listening to the Europeans. They are not listening to the vast majority of innocent, peaceful Sunnis who are greatly concerned about the collateral damage from their dumb bombs.

That said, we do have them in this political process that Secretary Kerry is leading. In that process, they are in the minority in terms of their perception of how long Assad should stay. So, the question is whether continuing to participate in that will bring the force of the majority to cause them to reevaluate their view.

Mr. TROTT. Ambassador Nuland, you said a few minutes ago that it will be difficult to get—and if I am putting words in your mouth incorrectly, please tell me—but, basically, I think you said that it will be difficult to get to a transitional government if Russia never gets on the same page with respect to our goals in Syria, and if that is a fair statement or if they never listen to us with respect to their military operations. So, assuming for the moment they never listen, we never get on the same page, what do we do then?

Ambassador NULAND. I don't think I quite characterized it the way you did. One thing that the Russians have said is that the Syria people should be in charge of their own future. So, the other piece of this that I think we have underplayed this morning, although I would defer to Assistant Secretary Patterson, is where the Syrian representatives, whether they are regime folk other than Assad or whether they are extremes of the opposition, want to take this, given the fact that the country is being torn apart by what is happening now.

Mr. TROTT. But, just looking down the road, if Russia doesn't want to ever move toward a transitional government, what do we do then?

Ambassador NULAND. Again, I think we can't project a straight line from here to there. We are increasing our support for the moderate opposition. We are raising the cost for hitting the wrong folk. We are trying to mobilize the rest of the international community to lean on the Russians. We will see. This thing is costing them. It is also costing them at home.

Mr. TROTT. Right. And I will yield back. But I think it is a mess. When we had good options, we didn't make a decision several years ago. And I think what someone said earlier today is exactly correct, which is we are just trying to run out the clock. And so, the next administration will inherent a situation in Syria that has Russia just as engaged as it is today and our options will be even more limited.

Thank you. I yield back.

Mr. PERRY. The Chair thanks the gentleman.

The Chair recognizes the gentleman from Florida, Mr. Yoho.

Mr. YOHO. Thank you, Mr. Chairman.

I appreciate you both being here.

I am amazed at the level of what appears to me—I have only been here for 3 years in Congress—but it appears to be a high level of incompetence, lack of strategy, lack of planning, and it is almost laughable, other than there has been over 250,000 Syrians slaughtered, the billions of dollars it has cost us, the risk to our military.

I look at this stuff, and I just want to go through a timeline since my time in Congress. Obama, August 2013, this administration was going to attack Syria and do no-fly zones. We sat at the White House. There was no strategy. They didn't have an estimate of the cost. Mr. McDonough, the Chief of Staff, said it would be over $1 billion a month. I asked him how long it was going to take. He said, estimated 10 years at $1 billion a month.

And we had just shut down. There was no authorization to go over there. We are attacking a sovereign nation without an AUMF.

President Obama went on to say there was a red line if Syria uses chemical weapons. They used it. There was no follow-through. They failed to act.

The President and John Kerry both said that Assad must go. Then, they denied it, said they didn't say that; the world said that.

John Kerry said there was no diplomatic solution to the chemical weapons problem in Syria. Yet, 2 weeks later after he said that, Russia jumped in there, showed leadership, and within 2 weeks there was an agreement to get rid of the chemical weapons. And I find it interesting that we didn't think that could happen. Yet, Russia brokered it, and we wound up paying for it.

The President said no boots on the ground multiple times. ''No boots on the ground.'' ''No boots on the ground.'' And then, we went with a $500 million to train, equip, and arm 5,000 to 6,000 vetted Free Syrian Rebel Fighters, whatever that is. And we find out a year later that is a complete failure. They have trained possibly 40 to 50, but only 5 made it to the field, at the cost of $50 million. That is $10 million a fighter. It has got to be laughable other than it is reality and it is just bad form.

I guess my question is, why hasn't the President worked to create the safe zones when especially the chairman of this committee, Chairman Royce, and Ranking Member Engel asked for that 4 years ago? Why has that not happened?

Ambassador PATTERSON. Because it is hugely difficult, complex, and——

Mr. YOHO. Okay, I am going to stop you there because you said that earlier today.

Ambassador PATTERSON. Okay.

Mr. YOHO. It is hugely complicated, difficult, expensive——

Ambassador PATTERSON. And resource-intensive.

Mr. YOHO. Resource-intensive.

Ambassador PATTERSON. Let me answer——

Mr. YOHO. I am going to stop you there because I want to add this. This is what I wanted you to bring out. It is complicated, extensive, very costly. How costly is it to have 4 million displaced refugees that have gone around the world that have disrupted the whole world as far as refugees just leaving there, 7.5 million displaced in Syria? That is pretty costly, too, isn't it? Isn't that disruptive?

Ambassador PATTERSON. That is costly and we are trying to contribute to alleviate that problem.

But let me talk in more detail about some of these safe zones/air exclusion zones. The Department of Defense has not proposed an option that does not have a very significant contribution/investment of U.S. air power. That air power would be diverted from the fight against ISIL. The fight against ISIL, which is an extraordinary virulent terrorist group, is a threat to us and our allies and the neighbors. So, that is the first priority.

It is also extremely difficult to patrol and to protect these safe zones on the ground, and that would require a very significant investment of ground forces of some sort. But the primary reason is the investment of air power.

Mr. YOHO. If we are going to attack this, we need to attack it. And then, the lack of diplomatic efforts or even a hint of that, over the last 3 years I have not seen it until Russia steps in there. And then, Russia puts in 2,000 troops, brings in the tanks, brings in all this armament. And we respond with 50 ground troops when the President said no American troops on the ground. This is an escalation. This is the beginning of an escalation of troops that are going to happen.

And my question to both of you is, why should I, or anybody on this committee or anybody in Congress, support anything this administration attempts with such a poor strategy of winning this. You know, the President doesn't even come out and acknowledge who we are fighting, ISIL, radical Islamic Jihadists. They won't even acknowledge that. Yet, we are going to kind of go at this and kind of do little efforts to try to defeat ISIL. I think it is a joke.

Again, my question is, why should I support anything this administration does in the Middle East, Syria, the Middle East, or even in the Ukraine, with the lack of strategy that I see?

And you were talking about how we have to protect Israel. But, yet, we have the Iran nuclear deal that does anything but protect Israel. Why should I support this, anything they are doing?

Ambassador PATTERSON. Well, I guess the short answer, Congressman, is that ISIL is a threat to us and to our European allies and to the neighbors in the region. And we are already seeing incursions by ISIL, pressure against Jordan and pressure against Saudi Arabia. I think that is the short answer. You have asked a much broader question, I think, but I think that is the short answer to your question.

Mr. YOHO. Well, if we are going to attack them, if we are going to do this, let's do it right and let's get a strategy, and let's make it count, instead of just kind of playing around with it. And I don't mean playing around with it because we have got troops on the ground, and I am sure if they are on the ground, they don't think they are playing.

I yield back.

Mr. PERRY. The Chair thanks the gentleman from Florida.

Without objection, I am pleased to recognize Mr. Jeff Fortenberry of Nebraska, a former member of this committee, who has remained engaged on these issues, and particularly the plight of Christians and other religious minorities in this region of the world.

Mr. Fortenberry.

Mr. FORTENBERRY. Thank you, Mr. Chairman.

Madam Ambassadors, welcome. I am sorry I didn't have the benefit of hearing the earlier conversation, but I do want to divert to the question that the chairman just laid out.

Before I do so, Ambassador Patterson, we met a number of years ago when you were in the Consulate at Peshawar, Pakistan. That was a few days before there was an assassination or a kidnapping attempt upon you. And then, from there, as I recall, you went on to become Ambassador in Pakistan as well as Egypt. So, I just want to thank you for your many years of dedicated service in very difficult areas.

I don't think we have had any interaction, Ambassador Nuland, but I appreciate both of your willingness to testify today.

One of the grave concerns in the Middle East is this, and let me divert for a moment by telling you a story. I happened to be in an audience with Pope Francis a little while back, and he was presented a small Christian crucifix. It was worn by a young Syrian man who was captured by the Jihadists, and he was told to convert and he refused, and he chose his own ancient faith tradition, Christianity. And he was beheaded.

His mother was able to recover his body and found the cross and fled and made her way to Austria, where she settled as a refugee. And through that means, one of the persons that I was with in this audience was able to present that to Pope Francis.

One of the more dramatic parts of this crisis that seems to come and go in regards to our attention is this deliberate, systematic attack on Christians and other faith traditions, including Yazidis and other religious minorities. And by the way, I have the largest Yazidi refugee population in America where I live in Lincoln, Nebraska.

Is this genocide?

Ambassador PATTERSON. I don't know the answer to that. I think that is a legal term. I think there will be some announcements on that very shortly.

Mr. FORTENBERRY. Well, I would appreciate both of your willingness to engage robustly on this topic. The reason is we have, as the chairman alluded to, introduced a resolution that does call this genocide. And while there are certain international legal implications from that, nonetheless, elevating the plight of Christians and other religious minorities in their own ancient homeland, including Syria which is approximately, Christians are about 10 percent of the population, raises the international consciousness of this and provides a gateway for further strategy around defense and security measures, as well as, once all of this, hopefully, in the future stabilizes, reintegration of those populations back into their rightful homelands.

And this is a very important, I think, gateway to use this resolution or the resolution is an important gateway for not only the discussion to elevate consciousness, but, again, a larger platform as to how to stabilize these areas and demand that the rich diversity of religious tradition that has existed in some of these areas be allowed to not only return, but flourish, as a part of any political or security settlement moving forward.

I think there are significant problems with this, obviously, in Iraq as well. We have been able to form a new burgeoning relationship with the Kurds who have been very respectful of religious plurality and have undertaken waves of immigration or refugee populations and absorbed that, as well as the Jordanians and the Lebanese. This is a very important components as we move forward an think through a strategy that actually brings about some stability and maybe a political settlement moving forward.

In this regard, there is another problem, however, that I would like to point out. It is my understanding that we have only admitted 53 Christians as refugees from the conflict in Syria. So, that is disproportionate, obviously, to the population size. Can you give any perspective on that, please?

Ambassador PATTERSON. My colleague Anne Richard was here with Mr. Rodriquez a few weeks ago to talk about refugee admission policy. And the numbers, I think we have admitted about, as of today, a little over 2,000 Syrians and we are planning to admit some more, of course.

They have to meet very strict vetting requirements and research into their particular circumstances and background. I don't have an answer why the Christians are underrepresented.

Mr. FORTENBERRY. Yes, I think one of the challenges is that Christians are generally not in refugee camps. So, they will be spread out through the population, whether it is in the basement of a relative or in some church basement or in some other circumstance versus cordoned into some definable entity like refugee camp. I think it is part of the problem. But, clearly, this segment of Syria's population is under grave stress, as are others.

Ambassador PATTERSON. Mr. Fortenberry, we entirely agree that these communities are under enormous stress. We have been in close contact with them through their religious leaders, both in country and their religious leaders here in the U.S. And we are very mindful of the points you make, that the most desirable outcome for them after thousands of years is that they be reintegrated into these countries and not dispersed.

And so, we try to work with these communities. We try to sustain them. But I will take your point back about the refugee admissions and get you an answer.

Mr. FORTENBERRY. Thank you very much, Mr. Chairman, for accommodating me today, and a pleasure to speak with you both. Thank you.

Mr. PERRY. The Chair thanks the gentleman.

The Chair also recognizes Mr. Engel.

Mr. ENGEL. Thank you very much. I know you have been here for a while. I was over at the White House with a series of appointments. But I did want to try to come here, not so much to ask questions, but to publicly compliment both of you. You are two of the most capable people I have had the pleasure of dealing with and meeting, hard-working and smart and tenacious, and all the nice things I can say about both of you. So, I want to just thank both of you for your service to our country. It really means a great deal when we can have people of your caliber and intellect and hard work and work ethic working for the United States of America. So, I just wanted to thank you.

I have treasured the times through the years that I have had the opportunity to speak with both of you in person, on the telephone, and everything else. So, just thank you.

I am sure everything has been covered, and I will read the script very, very carefully.

But neither one of you has ever said no to me when I needed to meet with you or ask you something. And so, just a very great, bipartisan thank you to both of you.

Mr. PERRY. The Chair thanks the gentleman.

The Chair would also like to thank the Ambassadors for being here. We know that you are sent here on a tough mission, and please don't take any of the remarks from the dias here as personal. We have a charge of oversight and to get the answers on behalf of our constituents. As you can tell, many of us on both sides of the aisle are very frustrated with the circumstances.

I do have one question before you pack it all up that I think a lot of people watch what is happening and they don't know the answer to this. Ambassador Patterson, you said—I think you were asked earlier about the refugee flow into Europe and why some of the Arab countries weren't doing more, except for paying to help ameliorate that. I think the sense was, why aren't they taking? Why aren't they taking some of or many of these refugees? I think your answer was they are very different societies and they don't accept, and so on and so forth.

With all due respect, it seems to me that Europe is a very different society than much of Arabia. Are we doing nothing? Do we have no plan? Do we have no interest in urging and pressuring and cajoling our Arab partners, so to speak, in the region bordering Syria particularly to take any of these refugees or do anything more than have them move lock stock and barrel across seas, dangerous journeys across land and mountains and cold, and everything a cultural difference for them into Europe? Is there no other effort in that regard?

Ambassador PATTERSON. Well, certainly, Mr. Chairman, there are efforts to encourage these countries to take in more refugees. It is not that hundreds of thousands of Syrians don't live in these countries. I think the issue for these countries is that a number of them have tiny domestic populations, and a population of foreigners, guest workers that are in some cases 8-to-10 times the local population. So, they are very reluctant to take in additional——

Mr. PERRY. But isn't that a similar circumstance in many of the European countries, the smaller ones, that the same exact circumstance is present at that moment? They are small populations currently, and they are being overrun. Their services are being overrun by people of a completely different culture and——

Ambassador PATTERSON. Yes. No, no, but, again, we have encouraged the Gulf countries to take in more refugees. And again, we have encouraged them to give generously to the U.N.——

Mr. PERRY. Is there any plan for more than encouragement, like some subtle pressure maybe, diplomatic pressure, economic pressure, pressure to help alleviate the situation? It seems fantastic to many of us that they are happy to help watch this inflow of humanity into Europe and take almost virtually none of it in themselves.

Ambassador PATTERSON. Well, again——

Mr. PERRY. And I know some of the countries in the region have, but some have not, and some of the larger ones have not.

Ambassador PATTERSON. Jordan and Lebanon and Turkey have taken millions of these refugees.

Mr. PERRY. Right, right. But there are other ones that border that have not taken.

Ambassador PATTERSON. Yes. And the other thing, I think the phenomenon we are seeing at this time now is that most of them prefer to join family members who have gone to these other countries. I actually do not think there has been such a draw for these refugees to resettle in the Gulf. Again, there are hundreds of thousands of Syrians——

Mr. PERRY. Well, if they are not welcomed in the Gulf and they are welcomed in Europe, after leaving a war—you know, once you decide to leave everything, I would imagine you would go where you feel more welcomed. But, if you are not welcomed at all in the neighboring countries, you are going to choose the best of your options, I would imagine.

And so, that is just a thought. And I think that a lot of Americans ask that question. So, I appreciate your answer. I would hope that the administration would do more, as much as it could to encourage our partners and allies in the region to do more than what they are doing in regard to physically taking those refugees.

And I thank you.

At this time, this hearing is adjourned.

[Whereupon, at 12:49 p.m., the meeting was adjourned.]

APPENDIX

MATERIAL SUBMITTED FOR THE RECORD

FULL COMMITTEE HEARING NOTICE
COMMITTEE ON FOREIGN AFFAIRS
U.S. HOUSE OF REPRESENTATIVES
WASHINGTON, DC 20515-6128

Edward R. Royce (R-CA), Chairman

November 4, 2015

TO: MEMBERS OF THE COMMITTEE ON FOREIGN AFFAIRS

You are respectfully requested to attend an OPEN hearing of the Committee on Foreign Affairs, to be held in Room 2172 of the Rayburn House Office Building (and available live on the Committee website at http://www.ForeignAffairs.house.gov):

DATE: Wednesday, November 4, 2015

TIME: 10:00 a.m.

SUBJECT: U.S. Policy After Russia's Escalation in Syria

WITNESSES: The Honorable Anne W. Patterson
                     Assistant Secretary
                     Bureau of Near Eastern Affairs
                     U.S. Department of State

                     The Honorable Victoria Nuland
                     Assistant Secretary
                     Bureau of European and Eurasian Affairs
                     U.S. Department of State

By Direction of the Chairman

The Committee on Foreign Affairs seeks to make its facilities accessible to persons with disabilities. If you are in need of special accommodations, please call 202/225-5021 at least four business days in advance of the event, whenever practicable. Questions with regard to special accommodations in general (including availability of Committee materials in alternative formats and assistive listening devices) may be directed to the Committee.

COMMITTEE ON FOREIGN AFFAIRS
MINUTES OF FULL COMMITTEE HEARING

Day _Wednesday_ Date _11/04/2015_ Room _2172_

Starting Time _10:08_ Ending Time _12:49_

Recesses _0_ (____to ____) (____to ____) (____to ____) (____to ____) (____to ____) (____to ____)

Presiding Member(s)

Chairman Edward R. Royce

Check all of the following that apply:

Open Session ☑   Electronically Recorded (taped) ☑
Executive (closed) Session ☐   Stenographic Record ☑
Televised ☑

TITLE OF HEARING:

U.S. Policy After Russia's Escalation in Syria

COMMITTEE MEMBERS PRESENT:

See attached.

NON-COMMITTEE MEMBERS PRESENT:

Rep. Jeff Fortenberry

HEARING WITNESSES: Same as meeting notice attached? Yes ☑ **No** ☐
(If "no", please list below and include title, agency, department, or organization.)

STATEMENTS FOR THE RECORD: _(List any statements submitted for the record.)_

SFR - Rep. Eliot Engel
SFR- Rep. Gerald Connolly

TIME SCHEDULED TO RECONVENE
or
TIME ADJOURNED _12:49_

Jean Marter, Director of Committee Operations

HOUSE COMMITTEE ON FOREIGN AFFAIRS
FULL COMMITTEE HEARING

PRESENT	MEMBER	PRESENT	MEMBER
X	Edward R. Royce, CA	X	Eliot L. Engel, NY
	Christopher H. Smith, NJ	X	Brad Sherman, CA
X	Ileana Ros-Lehtinen, FL		Gregory W. Meeks, NY
X	Dana Rohrabacher, CA		Albio Sires, NJ
X	Steve Chabot, OH	X	Gerald E. Connolly, VA
	Joe Wilson, SC	X	Theodore E. Deutch, FL
X	Michael T. McCaul, TX		Brian Higgins, NY
X	Ted Poe, TX	X	Karen Bass, CA
X	Matt Salmon, AZ	X	William Keating, MA
X	Darrell Issa, CA		David Cicilline, RI
	Tom Marino, PA		Alan Grayson, FL
X	Jeff Duncan, SC	X	Ami Bera, CA
X	Mo Brooks, AL	X	Alan S. Lowenthal, CA
	Paul Cook, CA	X	Grace Meng, NY
X	Randy Weber, TX	X	Lois Frankel, FL
X	Scott Perry, PA		Tulsi Gabbard, HI
X	Ron DeSantis, FL	X	Joaquin Castro, TX
	Mark Meadows, NC	X	Robin Kelly, IL
X	Ted Yoho, FL		Brendan Boyle, PA
X	Curt Clawson, FL		
X	Scott DesJarlais, TN		
X	Reid Ribble, WI		
X	Dave Trott, MI		
	Lee Zeldin, NY		
X	Dan Donovan, NY		

EDWARD R. ROYCE, CALIFORNIA
CHAIRMAN

AMY PORTER   THOMAS SHEEHY
Chief of Staff   Staff Director

ELIOT L. ENGEL, NEW YORK
RANKING DEMOCRATIC MEMBER

JASON STEINBAUM
Democratic Staff Director

One Hundred Fourteenth Congress
U.S. House of Representatives
Committee on Foreign Affairs
2170 Rayburn House Office Building
Washington, DC 20515
www.foreignaffairs.house.gov

Full Committee Hearing – "U.S. Policy in Syria After Russia's Escalation"
Statement for the Record

HON. ELIOT L. ENGEL

of New York

Wednesday, November 4, 2015

Mr. ENGEL. Mr. Chairman, thank you for calling this hearing. Developments in Syria over the last month have raised a range of new questions and concerns that I hope we can address today.

So I want to welcome our witnesses to the Foreign Affairs Committee. Secretary Patterson, Secretary Nuland, thank you for appearing here today. Thank you for your service. And thank you for your leadership dealing with two difficult regions during difficult times.

Where to begin with Syria?

At this point, the whole situation is such a mess that it might be tempting to throw up our hands and walk away. Let Russia deal with it. But then we're reminded of the daily toll of those lost to Assad's barrel bombs, at the hands of ISIS terrorists, or, most recently, to Russian attacks.

We're reminded of the photographer, known as Caesar, who sat in this room a year ago, showing us in searing, graphic detail what Assad has done to his own people. We're reminded of the millions of Syrian refugees, their lives shattered and their homes lost. We're reminded of the real security interests at stake for the United States and our partners in the region. And we're reminded that American leadership is most important in the most difficult situations, not the easy ones.

Several years ago, I favored a program to train and equip the moderate, vetted Syrian opposition. I wrote legislation that would have pursued that course.

That was early in the conflict when we had an opportunity to change the dynamics on the battlefield. It was before the death toll reached into the hundreds of thousands. It was before millions more spilled over Syria's borders, creating a refugee crisis that now spans two continents. It was before ISIS rose up as a brutal and destructive force in the region.

So by the time the United States finally enacted a train-and-equip effort, it was far too late. It was also too little. The mission was doomed from the start by its own limited parameters—training vetted rebels only to fight ISIS, while not fully understanding that they would rather oppose the Assad regime.

So where do we go from here?

Today, I hope we can get a clear view of our strategy going forward, and there are a few issues I'd like to focus on.

First, with the demise of the train-and-equip program, we've begun assisting forces that are already fighting ISIS. That's a good step. How can we get these groups what they need quickly and efficiently, and help ensure they are an effective fighting force? And how will the narrow, limited deployment of American Special Operations Forces contribute to this effort?

Next, I'm deeply concerned about Russia's growing involvement. I simply don't trust Putin. He's been driving a crisis in Eastern Europe for more than a year, and now he's sticking his nose into Syria. His goal is to keep Assad in power – a fact made clear by his targeting of the moderate opposition. How has Russia's involvement affected our strategy for Syria? And what impact is it likely to have on efforts to achieve a diplomatic resolution of the conflict?

Lastly, what is our strategy for helping deal with the massive refugee crisis? Half of the Syrian population has been displaced. The countries bordering Syria are shouldering a tremendous burden—countries that are already strained by threats to their security and stability. We need a long-term strategy, for the millions without a home and for an increasingly imperiled region. How are we working with countries in the Middle East to help ease the burden? What can we expect to see from our European allies? What changes are we considering in terms of refugees coming here to the United States?

I know these aren't easy issues, and there aren't any easy solutions. But nothing will be accomplished by hand-wringing or finger-pointing. Instead, lawmakers and the Administration should work together. We should find ways to strengthen the strategy, and provide whatever's needed to fully implement it.

And, critical to this effort: Congress should also do its job and pass a new authorization for the use of military force. For more than a year, we've stood by while the Administration relied on authorities from 2001 to carry out this mission. It's past time for the Congress to take action.

So let's learn from our past mistakes, look toward the future, and focus on new ways to move this crisis toward a resolution.

Again, I thank our witnesses, and I yield back.

Statement for the Record
Submitted by Mr. Connolly of Virginia

To date, U.S. policy in Syria has included a dizzying array of objectives and operations that have not always been consistent or worked in concert with one another. While removing Assad from power, preserving functioning state services and institutions, negotiating political space for the opposition, providing humanitarian relief, arming moderate rebel forces, and eliminating the Islamic State of Iraq and the Levant (ISIL) are all things we would like to see in Syria, they do not constitute a coherent strategy for unwinding the conflict and relieving human suffering.

The Syrian crisis is an immensely complex situation with several cross-cutting conflicts and multiple layers of humanitarian need, and the recent Russian escalation is yet another reminder that this conflict is further complicated by foreign stakeholders.

The recent dialogue convened in Vienna is an earnest effort to bring stakeholders, including Russia, to the table in order to articulate a shared path forward and devise a strategy to end large-scale violence in Syria. However, the effort seems plagued by the same lack of coordination and execution that has doomed similar efforts. While previous talks were hampered by competing expectations within the U.S. government, the opening round of Vienna II coincided with the Friday announcement that the U.S. would deploy up to 50 special operations forces into northern Syria. If this was a negotiating tactic, it seems an inconsequential commitment when measured against the presence Russia and Iran have on the ground. As a matter of new policy in Syria, it is an escalation of U.S. troop involvement that deserves careful evaluation.

If we are honest with ourselves, we must admit that the situation in Syria is in triage mode. With 250,000 civilians dead, more than 12 million Syrians displaced, and 4.1 million refugees fleeing Syria into surrounding countries and Europe, Syria is crumbling before our very eyes. The Syrian economy has contracted by as much as 75 percent and school attendance has been cut by more than 50 percent. The damage done to the demographics, economy, and education system in Syria will all but ensure that the detrimental impact of this crisis will be intergenerational.

We should immediately identify and address the greatest threats to the people of Syria and the stability of the region. We can and must prioritize immediate needs while maintaining strict objectives such as the removal of the murderous dictator Bashar al-Assad from power. To that particular end, it is promising to hear reports that Russia will no longer insist on President Assad retaining his position in Syria.

Regarding broader objectives in Syria, the participants in Vienna II released a Joint Statement that enumerates nine items on which the parties reached a mutual understanding. These include the need to preserve state institutions, support for a diplomatic resolution to the civil war, the imperative of defeating ISIL, and the pursuit of a nationwide ceasefire.

As Vienna II progresses, we should be mindful of our negotiating counterparts. While Russia commits rhetorically to the fight against ISIL, its airstrikes rain down on U.S.-supported opposition forces, and Iran has demonstrated immense resolve to support Assad's butchery. This distrust does not preclude a negotiated solution, but it necessitates a parallel U.S. policy that protects our partners in the region while talks are ongoing.

I look forward to hearing from our witnesses on how they would characterize the threats to regional stability and human life in Syria and how those threats might be prioritized. This seems to be the first step in developing a U.S. Syria policy that has some measurable impact on the lives of those affected by the crisis.